at HOME

Scrapbooking
with Faye Morrow Bell

CREATING
Keepsakes
SCRAPBOOK MAGAZINE

AT HOME | Scrapbooking with Faye Morrow Bell

Founding Editor	Lisa Bearnson
Co-founder	Don Lambson
Editor-in-Chief	Tracy White
Special Projects Editor	Leslie Miller
Associate Writer	Rachel Thomae
Copy Editor	Kim Sandoval
Editorial Assistants	Joannie McBride, Fred Brewer
Art Director	Brian Tippetts
Designer	Liz Craig Myers
Production Director	Gary Whitehead
Publisher	Mark Seastrand
Vice President, Group Publisher	David O'Neil

PRIMEDIA Inc.

Chairman	Dean Nelson
President & CEO	Kelly Conlin
Vice-Chairman	Beverly C. Chell

PRIMEDIA Consumer Media and Magazine Group

Chief Operating Officer	Daniel E. Aks
EVP, Consumer Marketing/Circulation	Steve Aster
SVP, Chief Financial Officer	David P. Kirchhoff
SVP, Mfg., Production & Distribution	Kevin Mullan
SVP, Finance	Kevin Neary
SVP, Chief Information Officer	Debra C. Robinson
VP, Manufacturing	Gregory A. Catsaros
VP, Direct Response & Classified Advertising	Carolyn N. Everson
VP, Single Copy Sales	Thomas L. Fogarty
VP, Manufacturing Budgets & Operations	Lilia Golia
VP, Consumer Marketing	Bobbi Gutman
VP, Human Resources	Kathie P. Malinowski
VP, Business Development	Albert Messina
VP, Database / e-Commerce	Suti Prakash

PRIMEDIA Outdoor Recreation and Enthusiast Group

SVP, Group Publishing Director	Brent Diamond
VP, Comptroller	Stephen H. Bender
VP, Marketing and Internet Operations	Dave Evans

COMPANY INFORMATION

For information on carrying *Creating Keepsakes* products in your retail store, please call 800/815-3583. For information on obtaining permission for reprints and excerpts, please contact the editorial assistant at *Creating Keepsakes* magazine in Bluffdale, Utah, at 801/984-2070. For information on ordering *Creating Keepsakes* magazine, call 888/247-5282. *Creating Keepsakes* is located at 14901 Heritagecrest Way, Bluffdale, Utah, 84065. Phone: 801/984-2070. Home page: *www.creatingkeepsakes.com.*

NOTICE OF LIABILITY

The information in this book is distributed on an "as is" basis, without warranty. While every precaution has been taken in the preparation of this book, neither the author nor PRIMEDIA Inc. shall have any liability to any person or entity with respect to any liability, loss or damage cause or alleged to be caused directly or indirectly by the instructions in this book.

TRADEMARKS

Trademarked names are used throughout this book. Rather than put a trademark symbol in every occurrence of a trademarked name, we state we are using the names only in an editorial fashion and to the benefit of the trademark owner with no intention of infringement of the trademark.

Printed and bound in the U.S.A.
ISBN 1 929180 54 3

HOME is where FAYE'S HEART is

by Lisa Bearnson

"Off 2 School"
Page by Faye Morrow Bell.

SUPPLIES
Canvas letters and metal accent: Li'l Davis Designs; *Ribbon:* Making Memories; *Ric rac:* me & my BIG ideas; *Computer fonts:* Times New Roman, Microsoft Word and Bondi, downloaded from the Internet; *Rubber stamps:* Making Memories and Postmodern Design; *Jump ring:* Making Memories; *Stamping ink:* VersaColor, Tsukineko; *Other:* Brads.

I'll admit it. I've been putting off scrapbooking these photos for almost three years. The reason? In my humble opinion, hot pink is one of the hardest colors to scrapbook with. I don't mind the color—I just don't love the results when I use it on my pages. The solution? I gave the photos to Faye Morrow Bell, and look how she solved the problem!

Notice how she *didn't* use hot pink on the layout—instead she "grounded" the bright colors in the photo with a neutral background. She also cleverly used the number "2" as a design element and added a few other embellishments.

This is why everyone's raving about hot designer Faye Morrow Bell—she designs her pages outside the box, going beyond the obvious. Her pages are very clean yet have an incredible sense of style. They're also very accessible—meaning they're easy to copy. Her love for family, tradition and values shine through on her pages.

Looking at the pages in this book is like taking a peek around Faye's home. Flavia once said, *"The beauty of family brings us cherished memories we wish to hold forever; for it is through our memories that our hearts find their way home."* Enjoy this unique book and best of luck capturing all those memories in the happiest place I know—home!

contents

chapter ONE | page 11

HOME is a place where you love your family

chapter TWO | page 35

HOME is the place where you always return

chapter THREE | page 55

HOME is where you share your values

chapter FOUR | page 75

HOME is a place where you celebrate with friends

chapter FIVE | page 97

HOME is where you celebrate who you are

what's a day like in YOUR LIFE?

Come in ...

Have you ever felt like something was missing from your scrapbook albums? I know I have. While it seemed as if I had no problem creating pages to celebrate holidays, birthdays and special occasions, I once struggled with what to do with photographs of my daily life. You know, the pictures of my daughter, Tyler, sitting in our backyard or the pictures of my best friend, Pansy, and I looking at magazines together.

In this book, I share my solutions for what to do with photographs that capture and communicate the details of our daily lives—the photos that reflect how we live, who we are and what we value.

I'm excited about sharing my ideas with you. Whether you want to tell your story with artistic techniques, beautiful photographs, heartwarming journaling or a combination of all of the above, you're sure to be inspired to capture the moments that mean the most to you. In this book, you'll learn how to:

- Design creative pages using "everyday" items
- Scrapbook "moment" photographs in a meaningful way
- Look at your daily life as a rich source of stories
- Explore your world for new design ideas
- Develop your own scrapbooking style with your favorite colors and page accents
- Share your favorite family stories in fresh and creative ways

Be Well,

"A Day in My Life"

Page by Faye Morrow Bell.

SUPPLIES

Textured cardstock: Bazzill Basics; *Transparency:* Creative Imaginations; *Ribbon:* Making Memories; *Computer fonts:* Typist and Kuenstler Script, downloaded from the Internet; Arial, Microsoft Word; CK Typewriter, "Fresh Fonts" CD, *Creating Keepsakes.*

AM
06:00
06:30
07:00
07:30
08:00
08:30
09:00
09:15
09:30

Come In...

7:30am
It's a Wednesday, so Tyler has weekday school. George is working from home this morning and then he's off to Wilson, North Carolina for a 2-day planning session.

4:30pm
Tyler suggests that we take a walk. I'm really in a design groove...but OK, we go walk. We had been walking for 20 minutes or so in the neighborhood when Tyler fell! It was her first scraped knee...no blood...just a scrape. But it really scared her, so she wailed and limped the entire walk home and asked that I take her to the hospital! I didn't have the heart to photograph her!

6:30pm
Quick dinner of salmon, rice and salad. Then Tyler and I watch TV, read the April CK that I received today and read books.

01:30
02:00
02:30
03:00
03:30
04:00
04:30
05:00
05:30
06:00
06:30
07:00
07:30
08:00
08:30
09:00
09:30
10:00
10:30
11:00
11:30

9:00am
I drop Tyler at weekday school and confer quickly with Amy Gruber, another parent. Amy and I are hosting the Valentine's Day party for the class this afternoon.

9:15AM
Photocopies at Alphagraphics, returns to Hobby Lobby and a new rolling briefcase bag from Office Max [I'm all set for this year's CKUs]

10:00AM
I've treated myself to an early 40th birthday gift...I've hired a fitness and nutrition coach for 6 months. Angela is awesome! We both celebrate that I lost weight while at HIA!

10:45am
Quick stop at Sam's Club to reprint the photo of Tyler that will be used on the cover of At Home: Scrapbooking with Faye Morrow Bell

11:30am
George meets me for lunch at Chick-Fil-A. I'll miss him the next couple of days!

Noon
The 10, 2-year olds are wired...they know there's a party today! I help the children construct a heart necklace using adhesive-backed foam. Amy brings cookies, vanilla frosting and red sprinkles. I think everyone had a great time!

2:30pm
While Tyler is napping I reply to emails [Rebecca Ludens @ About.com, Southern Lady Magazine, DIY Network, Jenni Bowlin and Sara Tumpane] and make a few quick calls to Creating Keepsakes. Designed a tag for the book using the new flowers by Making Memories and absolutely gorgeous ribbon from A Slice A Pie.

8:30pm
Tyler is still limping! I put her to bed and promised that her knee will be fine by morning.

9:00–midnight
Studio Time!

A DAY IN MY LIFE...
Wednesday 02-11-04

from the
HOME
— of —
Faye Morrow Bell

As a mother, I've discovered that one of my most important jobs is to guide my two-year-old daughter, Tyler, to be a good and loving person. One of Tyler's teachers recently told me how Tyler was kind to the shy new boy in her weekday school class. On several occasions, her teacher shared, Tyler would walk up to the new student and pat him on the back as if to say "come join us - it's okay."

Like Ralph Waldo Emerson, I believe that a key purpose in life "is to be useful, to be honorable, to be compassionate, to have it make some difference that you have lived and lived well." I hope that Tyler made a difference to the new boy in her class.

Faye

Tyler's nursery is a special place in our home. We've shared many special moments there as a family.

JOURNALING the intangible gifts

"Mommy"

SUPPLIES
Patterned paper: Scrip Scraps; *Textured cardstock:* Bazzill Basics; *Vellum:* The Write Stock; *Computer fonts:* Garamouche, downloaded from the Internet; 2Peas Beautiful, downloaded from *www.twopeasinabucket.com;* *Date stamp:* Office Depot; *Stamping ink:* Stampin' Up!; *Brads:* American Pin & Fastener; *Dog tag:* Chronicle Books; *Colored pencil:* Derwent; *Photo corners:* Canson; *Other:* Beaded chain.

A gift doesn't always have to arrive in a box with a big bow wrapped around it. What kinds of gifts have you received from your family members? A hug when you needed it most? A helping hand in the kitchen? Quiet time after a tough day at work? An hour of laughter while playing a game?

I created this layout for two purposes: to celebrate the day Tyler turned 18 months old and to record my feelings about a special gift she gave me that morning. My journaling reads as follows:

"When you awakened this morning, you stood up in your crib and began to sweetly sing, 'M-o-m-m-y, M-o-m-m-y!' When I opened the door of your nursery, you held up your arms, and with a huge smile said, 'Hey, Mommy!' You're eighteen months old today, but I'm the one who received the gift this morning."

"Rejoice"

SUPPLIES
Patterned papers: Pickle Press (music), 7 Gypsies (script) and Karen Foster Design (journaling); *Textured cardstock:* Bazzill Basics; *Ribbon:* C.M. Offray & Son; *Word rub-ons:* Making Memories; *Wax seal:* Creative Imaginations; *Pen:* Zig Writer, EK Success; *Other:* Chalk.

journaling with BOOKLETS

You can present journaling in many different ways on your pages. I often print my journaling directly on my background or print it on vellum, patterned paper or cardstock, then trim it to fit my page. Sometimes, though, a page calls for unique journaling.

An example is the tag booklet on the page at right. I printed my page title, "Some Things Never Change," on a smaller tag that also acts as the cover of my tag booklet. The inside tags read:

TAG 1 *"This wonderful photograph of Aunt Dorothy, Uncle Floyd and my cousin, Alfonza, was taken around 1945. At a family gathering in November 2003, I shared the photo with Alfonza and asked him what he remembers about it."*

TAG 2 *"He told me that he recalled being really excited about that tricycle. At three years old, Alfonza thought it was his to keep. How disappointed he was to learn that it was only a photographer's prop! Sounds just like Tyler 58 years later!"*

STEP-BY-STEP Here's one way to create a tag booklet with computer journaling:

1. Choose a tag template.
2. Use a ruler to measure the height and width of the tag you want to feature on your page.
3. In a word-processing program, draw a text box that is smaller than your tag.
4. Type your journaling inside the text box.
5. Print the journaling on cardstock or paper.
6. Place your template over the journaling. Trace and cut your tag.
7. Repeat as many times as desired to create a tag booklet.
8. Punch holes in the top of each tag and bind them together with ribbon, fibers, wire, key rings, twine—whatever you can think of.

VARIATION You can also print directly on pre-cut tags by setting up your journaling on your computer, printing a test page, positioning your tags over the printed areas with a light adhesive, then running the page through your printer a second time.

"Some Things Never Change"

SUPPLIES
Patterned papers and tags: 7 Gypsies; *Computer fonts:* Still Time, Mom's Typewriter and Vincent, downloaded from the Internet; *Ephemera:* Limited Edition Rubber Stamps; *Photo corners:* Nunn Designs; *Other:* Envelope and flower.

Some Things Never Change...

This wonderful photograph of Aunt Dorothy, Uncle Floyd and my cousin Alfonza was ... 1945. At a family gathering ... the photo with ... what he remembered ... ... he recalled being really ... At three years ... ... High. How ...

journaling ideas from YOUR HOME

"July 2001"

SUPPLIES

Textured cardstock: Bazzill Basics; *Computer fonts:* Fleurish Script and Copperplate Gothic, downloaded from the Internet; Times New Roman, Microsoft Word; *Punches:* EK Success and Marvy Uchida.

Looking for a different approach to journaling? Stop for a minute and look around your home. Where do you see your handwriting? Do you make notes on a calendar? Does your family communicate with each other via a phone message pad ("Faye, call your Mom!") or scrawl notes on a chalkboard ("I'll be back from taking Tyler to Kindermusik at noon.")? Perhaps you list your appointments on a calendar or in a date book.

Make a list of creative ways you can translate your daily lists and notes to your scrapbook pages (A faux chalkboard as a page element? A photocopy of your daily "to do" list? A mini-book made from a phone message pad on a page called "Messages to My Children"?).

I've always maintained some type of calendar or planner since I was in middle school. It's not surprising that I now use calendar elements on my scrapbook pages as well. I used a calendar for inspiration when I created this layout that celebrates the day-to-day events our family experienced during Tyler's birth month, July 2001.

On my second calendar page, I recorded a week's worth of events in Tyler's life. To create this page, I sewed pockets into patterned paper and tucked stamped and embellished journaling tags inside.

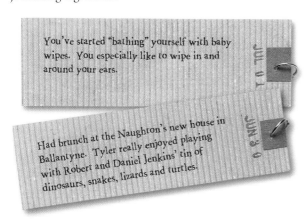

You've started "bathing" yourself with baby wipes. You especially like to wipe in and around your ears.

Had brunch at the Naughton's new house in Ballantyne. Tyler really enjoyed playing with Robert and Daniel Jenkins' tin of dinosaurs, snakes, lizards and turtles.

"Common Days"

SUPPLIES

Patterned papers: Design Originals (background and numbers) and Amscan (tags); *Textured cardstock:* Bazzill Basics; *Computer fonts:* Garamouche and Vincent, downloaded from the Internet; *Postage stamp:* Limited Edition Rubber Stamps; *Date stamp:* Office Depot; *Stamping ink:* Anna Griffin (red); Susan Branch (brown), Colorbök; *Clip:* Clipiola; *Jump rings:* Hirschberg & Schutz; *Ticket:* Collage Joy; *Other:* Negative.

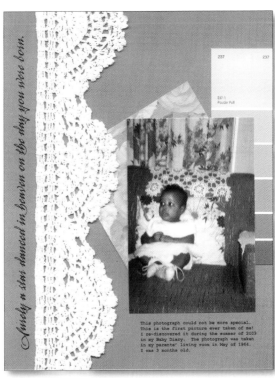

"First Photograph"

SUPPLIES

Patterned paper: Paper Pizazz; *Textured cardstock:* Bazzill Basics; *Computer fonts:* Arcana, Manuscript and Courier New, downloaded from the Internet; *Lace trim:* Wimpole Street Creations; *Other:* Paint chip.

journaling with MEMORIES from now and then

"Gloves"

SUPPLIES

Patterned papers: Cross-My-Heart (floral) and me & my BIG ideas (striped); *Textured cardstock:* Bazzill Basics; *Computer fonts:* Antique Type and Arcana Manuscript, downloaded from the Internet; *Date stamp:* Office Depot; *Stamping ink:* Susan Branch, Colorbök; *Ribbon:* C.M Offray & Son; *Eyelets:* Making Memories; *Other:* Gloves.

When Tyler's Aunt Sharon bought her this sweet pair of white gloves for Easter, I couldn't believe all the memories they stirred up for me. I decided to include the memories, listed below, on this scrapbook page.

• *New crisp hair ribbons* • *Dying Easter eggs* • *White patent leather shoes* • *Selecting a pattern and fabric with my mother for my Easter dress* • *Saying Easter speeches at church* • *Leaving home while it's still dark to attend Easter Sunrise Services* • *White straw hats* • *Easter egg hunts on Easter Monday … when Easter Monday was a holiday*

Journaling doesn't have to be chronological. Think about a time when a gift to your child, the smell of a favorite dish cooking or a certain song evoked a childhood memory that's special to you. Record these memories on layouts that celebrate who you are in relation to your family.

page BUILDING

My layouts are often heavily embellished. When selecting embellishments for my work, I ask myself both creative and technical questions. I start with a creative question: "What type of mood, feeling, theme or message do I want this layout to convey?"

My next step is to place my photographs on my design island and start pulling out an assortment of embellishments that might work for my page. When I created my "Just Wed" layout, for example, I knew I wanted to create a layout that conveyed joy, warmth and days gone by. I pulled out rubber stamps, lace, fabric-inspired paper, stickers, photo corners, a watch face, silk leaves, different colors of cardstock and an assortment of patterned papers.

After making my initial selections, I combine my photographs, my journaling and my accents onto a layout. I place my layout on my design island and literally take a giant step back from it. I like to see the layout as a "whole" instead of focusing on the individual elements. When evaluating whether my layout works or not, I look at the overall shape, balance and rhythm, and ask myself the technical questions: "Is it balanced? Is it unified? Does my eye move easily throughout the layout?"

If my answer is "yes," then my layout is complete. If my answer is "no," then I look for a specific design problem and move the elements around until the problem is solved.

"Just Wed"

SUPPLIES
Patterned paper: Anna Griffin; *Textured cardstock:* Bazzill Basics; *Computer font:* Vincent, downloaded from the Internet; *Watch face:* 7 Gypsies; *Other:* Lace and leaves.

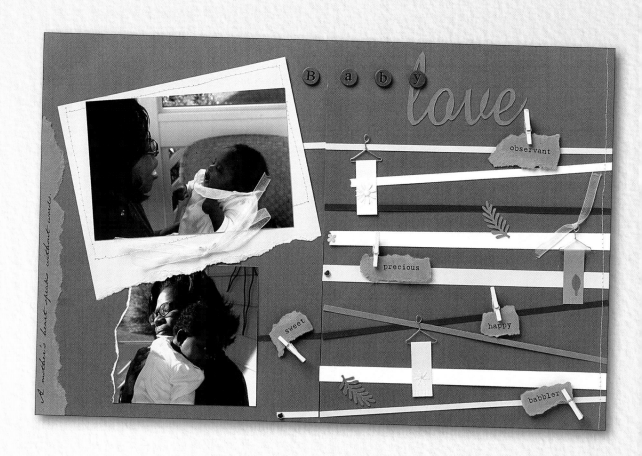

"Baby Love"

SUPPLIES
Textured cardstock: Bazzill Basics;
Computer fonts: Batik and Texas Hero,
downloaded from the Internet; *Eyelet
letters:* Magic Scraps; *Letter stickers:*
Making Memories; *Ribbon:* C.M. Offray &
Son; *Stickers:* Jolee's by You, Sticko by EK
Success; *Clothespins:* The Card Collection;
Brads: American Pin & Fastener; *Fern
punch:* Marvy Uchida.

scrapbooking with items that are MEANINGFUL to you

Have you ever had a family member who was known for her distinctive style? Perhaps it was your grandmother, who always dressed in classically beautiful dresses with matching hats, shoes and purses. Or maybe it was your great-aunt, who wore bright-red sweaters to every family party.

You can create a sense of style on your scrapbook pages by incorporating your hobbies and interests into your layouts. Take me, for instance. Sewing was my very first hobby. My mother is a wonderful seamstress, and as a young child, I loved to watch her cut and sew fabric. Believe it or not, at the young age of three, I was hand-stitching my own little purses. I love that I'm able to incorporate stitching, fabric and notions onto my scrapbook pages.

Stop for a moment and reflect on your former and current interests. How can you incorporate what you love to do onto your layouts? Did you love watercolor paints or sidewalk chalks as a child? Go ahead—play and have fun! Find a way to add the things you love to your pages and you'll soon start developing your own sense of scrapbooking style.

"I Will …"

SUPPLIES
Textured cardstock: Bazzill Basics; *Computer font:* Graverplate, downloaded from the Internet; *Accents:* Jolee's by You, Sticko by EK Success; *Corner charm:* Embellish It!.

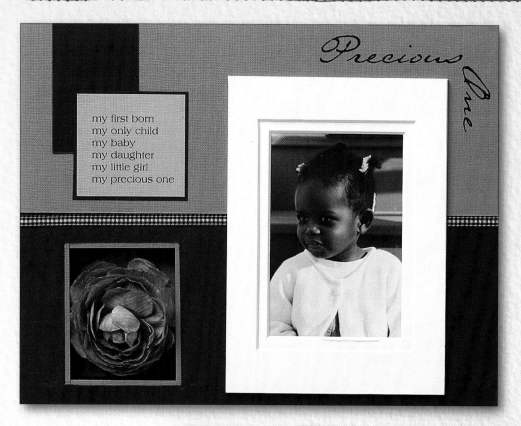

my first born
my only child
my baby
my daughter
my little girl
my precious one

Precious One

THE *World is your oyster*

smile
2000 remember

MARCH

SITTING AND FLITTERS AT THE LIBRARY

EATING CHEERIOS

SITTING ON YOUR OWN

FIRST PATENT LEATHER SHOES

and YOU, its

FLOWERS on your pages

"Precious One"

SUPPLIES
Textured cardstock: Bazzill Basics;
Computer fonts: Texas Hero and Amphion,
downloaded from the Internet; *Ribbon:*
C.M. Offray & Son; *Photo mat:* Spectrum;
Flower: Michaels.

VARIATION Another option for
flowers on your pages are the paper
flowers available from several scrapbook
companies. Here, I used the pansies from
Making Memories to make this tag.

"Our Family"

SUPPLIES
Patterned Paper: 7 Gypsies, Design
Originals; *Ribbon:* A Slice A Pie, Making
Memories; *Letter tiles:* Li'l Davis Designs;
Flower: Making Memories; *Concho:*
Scrapworks; *Other:* Eyelet.

"The World Is Your Oyster"

SUPPLIES
Patterned paper: Karen Foster Design;
Computer font: Top Secret, downloaded
from the Internet; *Overlay:* Artistic
Expressions; *Metal word, "2002" accent
and brads:* Making Memories; *"March"
tag:* EK Success; *"Remember" bubble:*
Li'l Davis Designs; *Map and postcard:*
me & my BIG ideas; *Other:* White paint,
flower, skeletonized leaf and burlap.

In her book *Living a Beautiful Life,* Alexandra Stoddard says, "Flowers
nourish a home." I just love flowers, both in my home and on my scrapbook pages, because they nourish my creative spirit. Roses, begonias and
hydrangeas are just a few of my personal favorites. Flowers add color,
dimension and a touch of simple elegance to any page.

STEP-BY-STEP On the layouts here, I've
presented silk flowers, available at craft
and discount stores, in two different ways.
Follow these easy steps to attach a flower
to your layout, as I did on my "The World
Is Your Oyster" page.

1. Trim the flower stem as close as possible
   to the petals. If you remove the entire
   stem, the flower will fall apart.

2. Punch a small hole in the middle of a
   metal-rimmed tag.

3. Insert the stem of the flower through
   the hole.

4. Apply E6000 adhesive between the stem
   and the tag. *Tip:* Be sure to apply ample
   adhesive. This adheres the flower to the
   tag and keeps it in an upright position.

5. Let the glue dry.

6. Attach the tag to your layout.

DESIGN TIP For my "Precious One"
layout, I cut a square in a piece of
foam-core board, glued the flower inside
the square, then covered the foam core
with cardstock.

Step 1

Step 2

Step 3

Step 4

folded POCKETS

Have you ever had the delightful experience of reaching into the pocket of a coat or a sweater you haven't worn for a year and finding a five-dollar bill, a little charm you thought you lost or an old movie stub that brings back memories of an enjoyable time with friends? Pockets are a wonderful place to hide little surprises, like special notes, photos, brochures, journaling, business cards and more.

STEP-BY-STEP I made the simple pocket on the layout at right with two layers of flat paper. Here's how to re-create this look:

1. Choose two coordinating sheets of 8½" x 11" paper. Look for a double-sided design for your pocket layer since both sides of your paper will show after it's folded. If you can't find a double-sided design you like, you can also glue two pieces of paper together.

2. Fold the right-hand bottom corner toward the middle of the paper. *See Figure 1.*

3. Fold the left-hand bottom corner toward the middle of the paper. *See Figure 2.*

4. This is your pocket. Embellish the pocket as desired with eyelets, rivets, fiber, ribbons and charms. *See Figure 3.*

5. Glue the pocket piece over your coordinating paper or cardstock. *See Figure 4.*

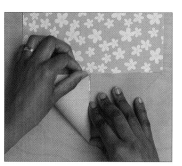
Figure 2

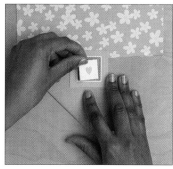
Figure 3

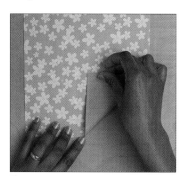
Figure 1

Figure 4

"Seventh Wedding Anniversary"

SUPPLIES
Patterned papers: Frances Meyer (brown), source unknown (green) and K & Company (leather); *Ribbon:* C.M. Offray & Son; *Eyelets:* Creative Imaginations; *Metal number:* Making Memories; *Computer font:* Monet, downloaded from the Internet; *Clip:* Target; *Other:* Jump ring.

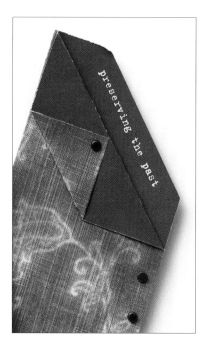

VARIATION You can trim your pocket layer to reveal more of the designs on the bottom layer.

George and I celebrated our 7th wedding anniversary at LaVecchia's Restaurant. The great food combined with a good bottle of wine and slow, easy conversation with my husband made for the perfect evening.

APRIL 29, 2002

Tyler and my mother have a beautiful relationship. Tyler refers to my mother as "Ma-ma". One of Tyler's favorite things is to have Ma-ma take her for a ride! My mother drives a Honda. At 25-months old, Tyler recognizes the Honda car symbol and constantly calls out from the backseat, "There's Ma-ma's car" as we run errands!

"Grandma"

SUPPLIES
Patterned paper: 7 Gypsies; *Textured cardstock:* Bazzill Basics; *Computer fonts:* Mom's Typewriter, Amphion, Tiles, Slalom, Arial, Ordner and Graverplate, downloaded from the Internet; *Ribbon:* C.M. Offray & Son.

word BLOCKS

A word block is a unique design element, and it's a simple yet effective way to communicate a lot of information in a fairly compact space. You can create a word block with a variety of fonts and colors. I use PowerPoint to create my word blocks, but you can do the same in almost any graphics program. Here's how:

STEP-BY-STEP

1. Open a text box and type in a word. Resize the text box if necessary.

2. Open a text box for each word you want to include in your word block. For example, if you want to include six words in your word block, you'll open a separate text box for each word. Vary fonts and colors as desired.

3. Click on each text box and rotate as desired. Arrange your words in an attractive shape to create a word block.

Step 1

Step 2

Step 3

VARIATION Think about creating word blocks with other elements as well. How about using stickers or tape labels? Why not collect signatures from your family members on strips of paper and make a signature word block? You can scan the signatures and manipulate them digitally, or you can arrange the strips of paper in an attractive fashion.

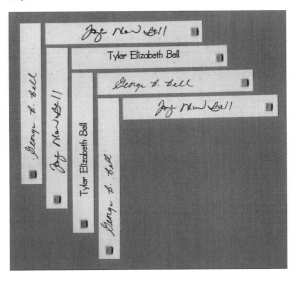

"Signature Block"

SUPPLIES
Textured cardstock: Bazzill Basics; *Computer font:* Second Grader, downloaded from the Internet; *Pen:* Zig Writer, EK Success; *Brads:* Making Memories.

spiral-bound FLIP BOOK layout

When I started scrapbooking these family photographs of my Aunt Dorothy's 80th birthday celebration, I knew I wanted to create something special. My initial thought was, "How can I include 14 photographs on this one-page layout?" I knew these pictures were too special and told too much of a story to eliminate even one of them.

The concept of telling a story led me to think about books and different methods for binding books. I suddenly realized I could create a unique layout by creating four photo flipbooks on one layout. Here's how:

STEP-BY-STEP I prepared my page, chose the photographs, printed journaling on cardstock and vellum, and brought my work-in-progress to my favorite copy store. They attached spiral binding on both sides of the layout so that the books flip open to both the left- and right-hand sides of the page.

This technique is a great way to preserve memories when you have quite a few photographs but don't want to create layouts for each set of pictures. Think about creating this type of book for a family reunion, a wedding, a holiday event, a birthday party and more. If desired, you could create a mini-cover with an open window to show just part of each photograph.

NOTE You'll probably want to use extra copies or digital prints when creating this type of booklet. I wouldn't use an original copy of a special heritage photograph with this technique, just in case.

"80th Birthday Party"

SUPPLIES

Patterned papers: Anna Griffin (floral) and Frances Meyer (background); *Vellum:* Bazzill Basics; *Bookplate:* Making Memories; *Computer fonts:* Texas Hero, Mom's Typewriter, Arcana Manuscript, Calisto and Typist, downloaded from the Internet; Times New Roman and Arial, Microsoft Word; *Twill:* 7 Gypsies; *Rubber stamp:* Postmodern Design; *Stamping ink:* Brilliance, Tsukineko; *Tag:* Avery; *Brads:* Doodlebug Design; *Other:* Wire binding.

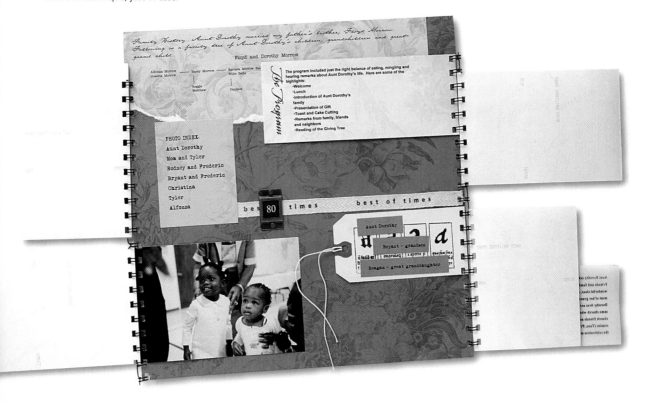

Family History...Aunt Dorothy married my father's brother, Floyd Morrow. Following is a family tree of Aunt Dorothy's children, grandchildren and great-grand child.

Floyd and Dorothy Morrow

The Program

The program included just the right balance of eating, mingling and hearing remarks about Aunt Dorothy's life. Here are some of the hig

80 best of times best of times

Aunt Dorothy celebrated her 80th birthday on November 1, 2003. Friends and family gathered at Ebeneezer Baptist Church in Derita on a wonderful clear, cool autumn Saturday. All of Aunt Dorothy's children, most of her grandchildren and her great-grand child attended. Aunt Dorothy lives across the street from my mother. And we all attended the same church when I was growing up. So it was wonderful to see old church friends and neighbors that I rarely see now. Additionally, several cousins (Teen, Preston, Vivian and Flatt) from New Jersey came home for the celebration as did my cousin, Priscilla, who now lives in Raleigh.

FAMILY

My maternal grandfather, Robert W. Moss, is shown here with his grandchildren in 1960. Better known as Papa, my grandfather eventually had twenty-five grandchildren.

ENVELOPE page backgrounds

"Family"

SUPPLIES

Textured cardstock: Bazzill Basics; *Stickers:* Nostalgiques, EK Success; *Trading stamps:* Collage Joy; *Rubber stamps:* Limited Edition Rubber Stamps (square design), Stampington and Company (calendar); *Stamping ink:* Susan Branch, Colorbök; ColorBox, Clearsnap; *Photo corners:* Canson; *Other:* Envelope.

I've always loved stationery, so it's only natural that I'm also fascinated with envelopes. Basic business envelopes, manila envelopes, decorated envelopes, vellum envelopes … they're all like treasure boxes, holding the promise of a small gift or a handwritten card. Did you know that envelopes are also a simple way to make unique page backgrounds?

On the layout at left, I lightly sealed a plain manila envelope and ran it through my printer to print the journaling on the lower-left-hand side. Next, I tore the envelope across the bottom-right-hand side, along the bottom and along a portion of the flap, then inked the torn edges. I mounted the envelope on black cardstock and balanced the design with colorful trading stamps.

VARIATION Save the handwritten envelopes you receive in the mail with birthday and seasonal cards. Use the envelopes, face-up, as a design element on your pages. You can also photocopy and reduce the size of the envelopes to include several on one page. What a great way to add your family members' handwriting to the scrapbook pages that celebrate the special occasions in your life!

"Report Card"

SUPPLIES

Patterned paper: Design Originals; *Textured cardstock:* Bazzill Basics; *Computer font:* Graverplate, downloaded from the Internet; *Photo corners:* Canson; *Other:* Eyelet and tape.

SLIDE MOUNT necklace

My daughter, Tyler, loves photographs almost as much as I do. She even has her own photo album that she proudly displays to friends and family. And she loves to pretend to take Mommy's picture!

One of Tyler's favorite things is a photo necklace I made for her. I reduced one of Tyler's favorite photographs by 75 percent (you can do this with photo-editing software or at your local copy store). Then, I placed the photo into a slide holder, embellished it, punched a hole and added a ribbon for wearing.

You can easily use a photo necklace as a page border. Choose three or four photographs, slip them inside slide holders and string them along the vertical or horizontal edge of your cardstock.

A photo necklace makes a great a party favor as well. Take digital pictures of each guest, reduce the size of each photo and print them on your color printer. Allow guests to decorate their own slide holders. Be sure to have an assortment of ribbon on hand so they can choose their favorite colors.

"Photo Necklace"

SUPPLIES
Word rub-ons and ribbon: Making Memories; *Slide holder:* Jest Charming.

VARIATION Instead of using sticky labels (you know, the old "Hello, my name is …") to introduce guests at a party, have guests make their own photo tags. Or, if you're going to meet up with your favorite group of online croppers at a scrapbook convention, you can choose a common color and/or decorating theme and easily identify your group members at the show.

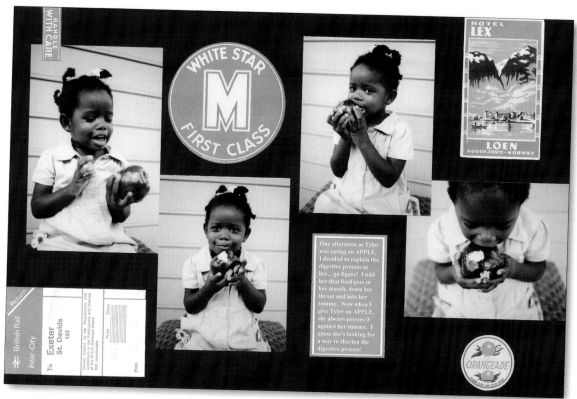

"Eating Apples"

SUPPLIES
Textured cardstock: Bazzill Basics;
Computer font: Times New Roman,
Microsoft Word; *Ephemera:* Rubber
Baby Buggy Bumpers, me & my BIG
ideas and Collage Joy.

One of my favorite things to do is shop for scrapbook supplies. I probably have enough supplies for five women! Here's a list of my favorite scrapbook and non-scrapbook stores:

All My Memories
Draper, Utah
www.allmymemories.com

Lowe's
www.lowes.com

Memory Lane
Gilbert, Arizona
www.memorylanearizona.com

Memory Lane Paper Company
Orem, Utah
www.memorylanepaper.com

Office Depot
www.officedepot.com

Scrapbooks 'n More
Kannapolis, North Carolina
www.scrapbooksnmorenc.com

Stampin' Grounds
Goose Creek, South Carolina
www.stampingrounds.com

Dollar stores

Fabric shops

We have white plantation shutters throughout our home. Yes, they are very practical, but I also love them because they remind me of the island we love to visit in the summertime.

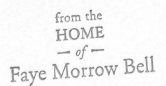

from the
HOME
— of —
Faye Morrow Bell

I love venturing out with my husband and daughter. It's so much fun introducing Tyler to "firsts" - first trip to the beach, first basketball game, first circus. But it has been even more fulfilling to have her ask to return home. She'll say, "I want to go to Mommy and Daddy and Tyler's house." My observation has been that she's not hungry or sleepy... she just loves the three of us playing together at home.

It seems as if Tyler has learned what eighteenth century author Jane Austen phrased so well, "there is nothing like staying at home for real comfort."

Faye

CAMERA creativity

"Tylermobile"

SUPPLIES
Textured cardstock: Bazzill Basics; *Map:* Hot Off The Press; *Compass:* Just Joshin'/Joshua's; *Computer fonts:* Texas Hero and Xerox, downloaded from the Internet; Courier New, Microsoft Word.

Photography is one of my favorite hobbies, and when I was introduced to the lomograph camera (the Action Sampler) in a photography class, I couldn't wait to try it out. My lomograph camera has four lenses. I click the shutter once, and the camera captures four slightly different images (see the pictures I've included here). The images are returned on one print and can be used as one image or cut apart and pieced back together on a scrapbook page. For my Tylermobile page, I took shots of our Volvo with my lomograph camera. To learn more, visit *www.lomography.com* or check your local camera store.

You can achieve a similar effect with some digital cameras. Check your digital camera user guide to see if your camera has a "continuous shot" function. The lens will click automatically for a certain number of shots, and then will piece the individual images into one photograph.

In addition to my lomograph camera, I occasionally use a panoramic camera for a different point of view. (You can read about my favorite films and cameras in "Faye's Favorites" at the end of this chapter.)

The lomograph camera captures four different images in one shot.

You can use all four shots together, or cut them apart and use them separately.

color photographs on TRANSPARENCIES

Believe it or not, this page is simply a photograph color-copied onto a transparency and attached between two layers of cardstock, which are held together with foam dots. I didn't manipulate the photograph with computer software at all. Instead, I waited for just the right moment to capture Tyler and her shadow on the beach.

I discovered that late afternoon is the best time to take strong shadow shots. As the sun sinks lower in the sky, the light becomes warmer and less harsh than the midday sun. Afternoon and evening sun also casts longer shadows, allowing you to design a more interesting photograph.

Original photograph

"My Shadow"

SUPPLIES
Patterned paper: 7 Gypsies (script);
Aluminum tag: Limited Edition Rubber
Stamps; *Brads:* American Pin & Fastener;
Steel stamp sets: Harbor Freight; *Other:*
Transparency and black patterned paper.

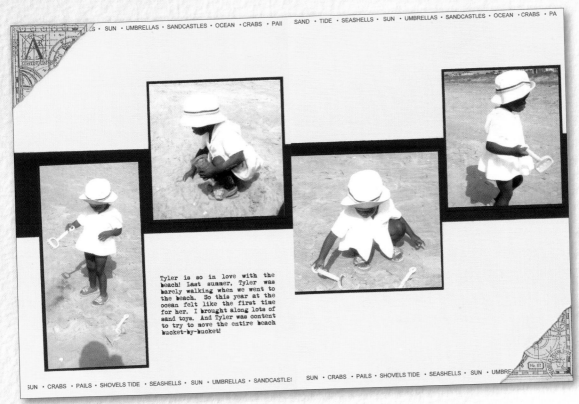

SAND · TIDE · SEASHELLS · SUN · UMBRELLAS · SANDCASTLES · OCEAN · CRABS · PA

Tyler is so in love with the beach! Last summer, Tyler was barely walking when we went to the beach. So this year at the ocean felt like the first time for her. I brought along lots of sand toys. And Tyler was content to try to move the entire beach bucket-by-bucket!

"Tyler in Love with the Beach"

SUPPLIES

Textured cardstock: Bazzill Basics; *Rubber stamp:* Stampers Anonymous; *Stamping ink:* Stampin' Up!; *Computer fonts:* Arial, Microsoft Word; Mom's Typewriter, downloaded from the Internet.

"Wild Dunes Resort— Summer 2003"

SUPPLIES

Textured cardstock: Bazzill Basics; *Patterned paper:* Karen Foster Design; *Metal frame and plaque:* Making Memories; *Punch:* The Punch Bunch; *Starfish charms:* JewelCraft; *Ephemera:* Collage Joy; *Computer font:* Trash, downloaded from the Internet; *Other:* Eyelet tape and jump rings.

ALTERED books

My husband, George, and I have been in love with Wild Dunes Resort since our first visit in 1999. We now visit several times each summer. We couldn't ask for more—it's an easy 3½-hour drive from Charlotte. And Wild Dunes is a beautiful 1,600-acre oceanfront resort surrounded by the Atlantic Ocean and the Intercoastal Waterway. That means two miles of pristine beaches.

We love spending lazy days lounging and walking on the beach, reading, eating at the local seafood restaurants and enjoying the many activities planned by the resort. We also enjoy visiting the local Barnes & Noble bookstore. In my opinion, it ranks second only to the Barnes & Noble I've visited in San Francisco.

I spotted this beautiful book on the clearance table during our August 2003 visit and knew immediately I would buy it. The watercolor sketches and script font really drew me in. I knew the book would inspire me, and I haven't been disappointed!

"Roses Book"

SUPPLIES

Vellum: Bazzill Basics and The Write Stuff; *Tags:* DMD, Inc.; *Fabric tags:* me & my BIG ideas; *Word rub-ons, metal letters, square brads, eyelet tops, bookplate and black ribbon:* Making Memories; *Photo corners:* Canson; *Chalk:* EK Success; *Black brads:* American Pin & Fastener; *Conchos and words:* 7 Gypsies; *Definitions:* FoofaLa; *Bookplate and safety pin:* Li'l Davis Designs; *Acrylic paint:* Plaid; *Pens:* Zig Writers, EK Success; *Computer fonts:* Courier, Microsoft Word; Mom's Typewriter and Top Secret, downloaded from the Internet; CK Cursive, "The Best of Creative Lettering" CD Vol. 2, *Creating Keepsakes; Other:* Brown brads, ribbon, fabric swatch and staples.

DIARY OF A ROSE LOVER

By Henri Delbard

Watercolors by Fabrice Moireau

'Grand Siècle'
The quintessential ROSE!
Feminine, elegant, beautiful—
a true rose color that is
exceptionally rich. I always begin a
"tasting" of scents with 'Grand Siècle'
because of its predominantly floral
perfume. It is the rose par excellence! Our sew...
and in the case of smell, as in hearing...

I spent my entire professional career working in Uptown Charlotte....almost fifteen years. But it was only on a recent Sunday afternoon visit with a friend that I took the time to really "see" uptown.   07/27/03

"Seeing Uptown"

SUPPLIES

Textured cardstock: Bazzill Basics; *Rubber stamp:* Inkadinkadoo; *Stamping ink:* Anna Griffin; *Computer font:* Tahoma, Microsoft Word.

taking the time to SEE

We live life at such a harried pace, it often seems as if we spend most of our days *looking* instead of *seeing*. It's amazing to me how my perception changes when I slow my pace. Only then am I truly able to see … and to feel. Colors seem deeper and richer when I begin to notice details I've never noticed before.

I've discovered that an easy way to get a quick energy boost is to take a deep breath, slow down and spend a few minutes observing everyday objects with a fresh eye—a tree, a garden, the exterior of your home, a loved one's face or your favorite room bathed in late-afternoon sun.

On this page, I captured what I "saw" on a trip to Uptown Charlotte, a place where I spent my entire professional career, almost 15 years. But it was only on a relaxing Sunday afternoon visit with a friend that I took the time to really "see" uptown.

Why not take your camera and re-visit a place you've spent a lot of time? Challenge yourself to capture as many small details as possible. When you scrapbook the photographs, include your feelings about the experience.

"Built in 1929"

SUPPLIES
Patterned papers: 7 Gypsies, Anna Griffin and Karen Foster Design; *Ruler:* Nostalgiques, EK Success; *Rubber stamps:* Stampin' Up! and Stampers Anonymous; *Stamping ink:* VersaMark, Tsukineko; *Brads:* American Pin & Fastener; *Jute:* Halcraft; *Photo corners:* Canson; *Computer font:* Mom's Typewriter, downloaded from the Internet; *Other:* Cardboard.

relax, respite and RETREAT

As a harried and hurried consultant, I was pleased to discover the beautiful sanctuary at St. Peter's Episcopal Church in Uptown Charlotte. Each season, the parish offers a series of chamber music concerts during lunchtime. These concerts became my own personal respite, a place where I could retreat with lunch from a nearby restaurant and relax in 45 minutes of solitude each Tuesday.

We all have places where we like to go to rest and relax. What are your favorite places to find solitude and comfort? Make a list of the places you go to recharge your creative batteries. Take photographs and include them in your scrapbooks as a reminder to yourself and your loved ones of the importance of taking time to rest.

"Rest"

SUPPLIES
Textured cardstock: Bazzill Basics; *Patterned paper:* Penny Black; *Ribbon:* C.M. Offray & Son; *Bell:* Westrim Crafts; *Letters:* Krafty Korner; *Photo corners:* Canson; *Computer fonts:* Vincent and Graverplate, downloaded from the Internet; *Other:* Vellum.

"Greenway"

SUPPLIES
Textured cardstock: Bazzill Basics; *Transparencies:* Magic Scraps; *Brads:* American Pin & Fastener; *Label maker:* Dymo; *Computer font:* Boston, downloaded from the Internet.

St. Peter's Episcopal Church HAS A BEAUTIFUL SANCTUARY IN UPTOWN CHARLOTTE. EACH SEASON, THE PARISH WOULD OFFER A SERIES OF *chamber music concerts* DURING LUNCHTIME. WHAT AN INCREDIBLE *respite* THAT BECAME FOR ME AS A HARRIED AND HURRIED CONSULTANT. I WOULD GRAB A LUNCH TO GO FROM A NEARBY RESTAURANT AND *retreat* TO ST. PETER'S FOR 45 MINUTES OF *solitude* EACH TUESDAY.

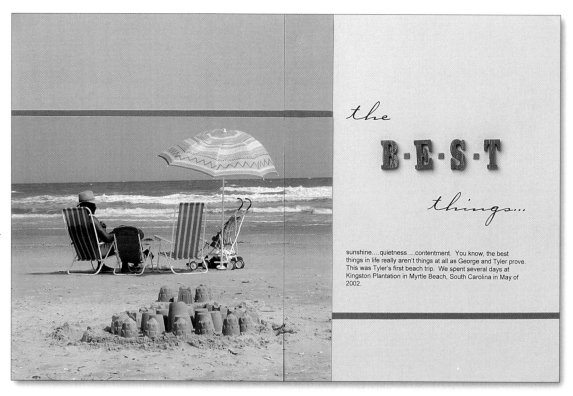

the
B·E·S·T
things...

sunshine....quietness....contentment. You know, the best things in life really aren't things at all as George and Tyler prove. This was Tyler's first beach trip. We spent several days at Kingston Plantation in Myrtle Beach, South Carolina in May of 2002.

"The Best Things"

SUPPLIES
Textured cardstock: Bazzill Basics; *Brads:* Making Memories; *Red letters:* Li'l Davis Designs; *Computer fonts:* Carpenter, downloaded from the Internet; Arial, Microsoft Word.

Long walks on the greenway in our neighborhood have become the highlight of our spring weekends!

Dandelion Blowing 101

this particular Sunday in April, George owed Tyler how to pick wildflowers. Of urse the highlight was learning how to blow e dandelions.

"Dandelion Blowing 101"

SUPPLIES
Textured cardstock: Bazzill Basics; *Vellum:* The Write Stock; *Bulldog clip:* Office Depot; *Eyelet:* Creative Imaginations; *Computer fonts:* Boston and Mom's Typewriter, downloaded from the Internet; *Other:* Skeletonized leaf, feathers and leather cording.

"Faye and Debbie"

SUPPLIES

Textured cardstock: Bazzill Basics;
Bookplate: Two Peas in a Bucket;
Fabric label: me & my BIG ideas;
Silver eyelet: Making Memories;
Silver sun tag: Chronicle Books;
Brads: American Pin & Fastener;
Black jump ring: Junkitz; *Pen:* Zig
Writer, EK Success; *Computer fonts:*
Mom's Typewriter and Texas Hero,
downloaded from the Internet;
Other: Ribbon and sun charm.

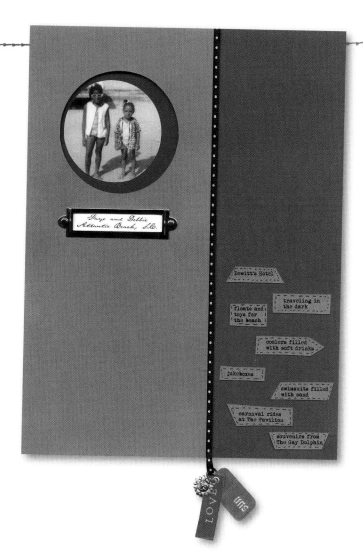

"Best of Times"

SUPPLIES

Patterned papers: Anna Griffin and
Frances Meyer; *Vellum:* Bazzill Basics;
Brads: Doodlebug Design; *Bookplate:*
Making Memories; *Twill:* 7 Gypsies;
Tag: Avery; *Rubber stamp:* Postmodern
Design; *Stamping ink:* Brilliance,
Tsukineko; *Computer fonts:* Texas Hero,
Mom's Typewriter, Arcana Manuscript,
Calisto and Typist, downloaded from the
Internet; Times New Roman and Arial,
Microsoft Word; *Other:* Wire binding

JULY 20 2003 · CHARLOTTE COLISEUM · THE STING

Tyler attended her first professional sporting event this summer. She and George and I saw the Charlotte Sting (Women's National Basketball Association) play the Cleveland Rockers. As usual, Tyler was well-behaved and attentive. Her favorite part was when the organist played and the crowd sang "If You're Happy and You Know It, Clap Your Hands"!

CHARLOTTE STING BASKETBALL · 2003 SEASON

BASKETBALL NET as a page accent

"Charlotte Coliseum"

SUPPLIES

Patterned paper: Amscan; *Textured cardstock:* Bazzill Basics; *Basketball photo:* Shotz by Danelle Johnson, Creative Imaginations; *Label maker:* Dymo; *Computer fonts:* Sadelle, downloaded from the Internet; Courier New, Microsoft Word; *Other:* Jump rings and basketball net.

When I had the idea to add a basketball net to a layout, I thought the net would cost me 10 or 15 dollars. When I discovered this basketball net at Wal-Mart for less than two dollars, I was delighted.

To add the basketball net to my page, I first trimmed it so I could layer it over the Shotz basketball photograph. I looped the net through jump rings, then used a tiny punch to punch holes in the label. I attached the jump rings through the holes, which hold the net in place.

The next time you're at a sporting event, consider looking for non-traditional accents you can use on a scrapbook page.

"May 2002"

SUPPLIES

Textured cardstock: Bazzill Basics; *Tag:* DMD, Inc.; *Stamping ink:* VersaMark, Tsukineko; *Computer fonts:* Garamouche, Graverplate, Wayne's Hand, Hanford's Hand, Trasks Hand, Ticket Capitals, Trebuchet, Patricia's Hand, Gail's Hand, Ordner, Wendy's Hand and Batik, downloaded from the Internet; *Other:* Foam stamp, tassel, postage stamp and ephemera.

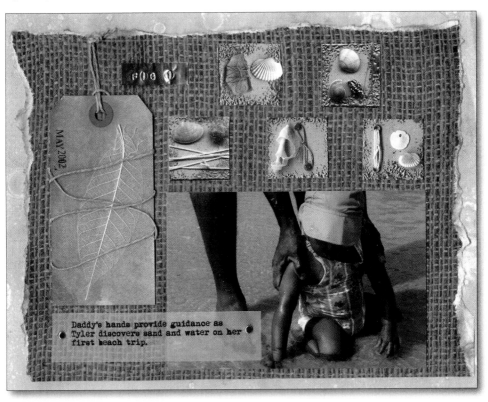

Daddy's hands provide guidance as Tyler discovers sand and water on her first beach trip.

EXPLORE your world for design ideas

One of Tyler's favorite places is the playground at the park. I'll admit it—I think I love the playground just as much as Tyler! Not only do I get to enjoy spending time with my daughter, but I'm also inspired by all the design ideas the park offers. Being at the playground is like being inside a great, big idea book full of colorful curves, long lines and fantastic frames.

After discovering a design idea at the park, try translating it to a scrapbook page. On this layout, notice how Tyler is framed by the slide's circular opening. The rivets on the outside of the slide could easily be re-created with eyelets, brads or even rivets on a scrapbook page. I computer-journaled my title with a font that mimics the look of wire mesh, and added actual mesh to two additional places on my layout: on my accent block and behind the torn cardstock on the upper-right-hand side of the layout. Notice how the layout flows up from the eyelets, around the photograph of Tyler and through the title letters.

DESIGN TIP: Look at the colors of cardstock featured in my picture block. The inside of the slide is the same color as the cardstock used under my accent block. By repeating this color from the photograph, the middle section of the layout seems like one unified section instead of three separate parts.

"Explore"

SUPPLIES
Textured cardstock: Bazzill Basics; *Screen wire:* Elgar Products; *Eyelets:* Magic Scraps; *Brad:* American Pin & Fastener; *Clock accent:* Jolee's by You, Sticko by EK Success; *Computer fonts:* Texas Hero, Mom's Typewriter, Ordner, Batik, Antique Type, Tilez and Graverplate, downloaded from the Internet; Arial, Microsoft Word; *Computer program:* WordArt; Microsoft Word.

"Family Vacation Memories"

SUPPLIES

Textured cardstock: Bazzill Basics; *Patterned paper:* K & Company; *Twill tape:* 7 Gypsies; *Staples:* Making Memories; *"Reflection" bubble:* Li'l Davis Designs; *Date stamp:* Office Depot; *Stamping ink:* Brilliance, Tsukineko; *Ephemera:* me & my BIG ideas; *Pen:* Zig Writer, EK Success; *Computer fonts:* Top Secret and Mom's Typewriter, downloaded from the Internet; *Other:* Negative and brochure cover.

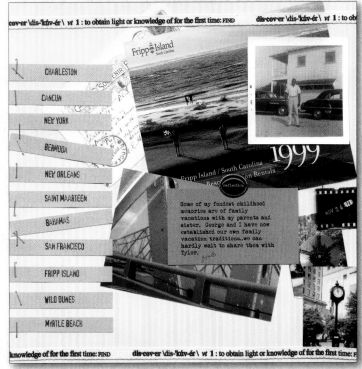

Am I Afraid?..
ABSOLUTELY!!

JUL 14 2003

I've always been afraid to ride roller coasters with big hills and dips. And this wooden coaster appears even more menacing from underneath! I've only ridden a big roller coasters once. For eighth-grade graduation, our class went to Carowinds, our local amusement park. Well, I wouldn't let me classmates see me sweat...I rode everything! Thank goodness for maturity and better judgment!

"Am I Afraid?"

SUPPLIES

Textured cardstock: Bazzill Basics; *White copier paper:* Xerox; *Stamping ink:* Anna Griffin; *Eyelets:* Making Memories; *Wire:* Amaco; *Computer fonts:* Trash, downloaded from the Internet; Courier New, Microsoft Word.

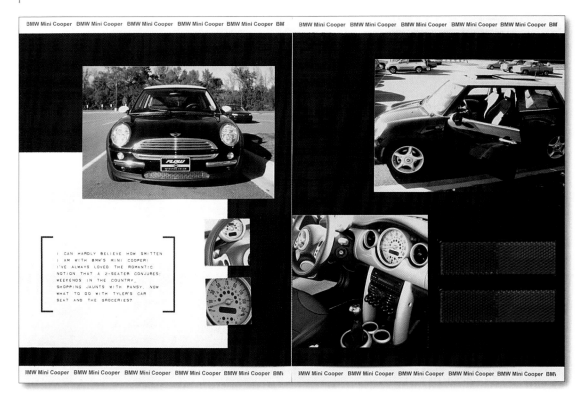

I CAN HARDLY BELIEVE HOW SMITTEN
I AM WITH BMW'S MINI COOPER!
I'VE ALWAYS LOVED THE ROMANTIC
NOTION THAT A 2-SEATER CONJURES:
WEEKENDS IN THE COUNTRY,
SHOPPING JAUNTS WITH PANSY. NOW
WHAT TO DO WITH TYLER'S CAR
SEAT AND THE GROCERIES?

"BMW Mini Cooper"

SUPPLIES
Textured cardstock: Bazzill Basics;
Computer fonts: Arial, Microsoft Word;
Ordner Inverted, downloaded from
the Internet.

Here's a list of my favorite cameras and photography supplies:

Black-and-White Film
Ilford Super 400-C41

Color Film
Kodak Gold 200

Photo Processor
Sam's Club

Cameras
Canon Rebel 2000 (SLR). I love this camera because of the high-quality photos it takes. I use it with the Ilford black-and-white film for shooting most of my black-and-white pictures. Also, if I'm looking for effects, like blurring the background or panning, this is my camera of choice. Because the Canon Rebel is manual, it offers me the most control and the most opportunity to be creative with my photography. In addition to the camera body, I have a normal lens (28-80mm) a zoom lens, a wide-angle lens and an electronic flash.

Olympus Camedia C-3040 (digital). This high-quality digital camera is perfect when I need instant feedback, for example, when I need to know if I've captured the right shot. Last Christmas I took test shots of our Christmas card photo of Tyler with the digital camera. After checking the lighting and the composition of my photographs, I took the final version with my SLR.

Pentax Optio S (digital). This camera is amazing! It's so tiny, it literally fits in an Altoids box. I carry it in my purse so I never miss a shot. It's well protected in the Altoids tin, so I've been known to stick it in my pocket and go!

from the
HOME
— of —
Faye Morrow Bell

My Guiding Principles :
1. God first
2. Learn the lesson
3. Always intend good

Faye

The Porch

George and I love sharing our evenings together on the porch. Cool breezes, starry skies and singing tree frogs provide the backdrop. Time seems to stand still as we spend hours talking, listening to our favorite music, reading and reflecting.

I expressed my APPRECIATION for the seasons with a simple black-and-white photograph, a bit of rubber stamping, a clock hand and the quote, "Winter is an etching, spring a watercolor, summer an oil painting, and fall is a mosaic of them all."

"Seasons"

SUPPLIES
Textured cardstock: Bazzill Basics; *Rubber stamps:* Postmodern Design (clocks), Anita's Stamps (fern leaves), Impression Obsession (small maple leaves), Stampin' Up! (medium), StampCraft (small); *Stamping ink:* VersaMark, Tsukineko; *Brads:* American Pin & Fastener; *Computer fonts:* CK Cursive, "The Best of Creative Lettering" CD Vol. 2, *Creating Keepsakes*; Garamouche and Copperplate Gothic, downloaded from the Internet; 2Peas Cookie Dough and 2Peas Rustic, downloaded from *www.twopeasinabucket.com*.

"Clever One"

SUPPLIES
Textured cardstock: Bazzill Basics; *Patterned papers:* Karen Foster Design, Design Originals and 7 Gypsies; *Computer font:* Courier New, Microsoft Word.

A wonderful way to share your values on your pages is with favorite quotes. The quote I used on this page simply reads, "When you BELIEVE, you open the door to wondrous possibilities."

When you believe

you open the door to wondrous possibilities

JANUARY 2003

"When You Believe"

SUPPLIES

Textured cardstock: Bazzill Basics; *Patterned paper:* Karen Foster Design; *Eyelets:* Doodlebug Design; *Rubber stamps:* Stampin' Up!, All Night Media and Inkadinkadoo; *Stamping ink:* Stampin' Up!; *Pen:* Zig Writer, EK Success; *Computer fonts:* Graverplate, Texas Hero and Garamouche, downloaded from the Internet; *Other:* Ribbon.

I look for quotes online at sites such as *www.twopeasinabucket.com, www.bartleby.com* and *www.brainyquote.com.* I've maintained quote journals for years; when I hear or read a quote I like, I jot it down in my small leather quote journal.

"Now and Forever"

SUPPLIES

Patterned papers: 7 Gypsies and Karen Foster Design; *Grid:* Déjà Views, The C-Thru Ruler Co.; *Tag and watch face:* 7 Gypsies; *Postage stamp:* Limited Edition Rubber Stamps; *Metal numbers and word rub-ons:* Making Memories; *Tickets:* Collage Joy; *Eyelets:* Magic Scraps; *White acrylic paint:* Plaid; *Ribbon:* C.M. Offray & Son; *Pen:* Zig Writer, EK Success; *Computer font:* Mom's Typewriter, downloaded from the Internet; *Other:* Jute.

What a wonderful example of love and COMMITMENT my mother and father shared with me. They were wed on December 21, 1952. My parents had been married 47 years when my father passed away in the spring of 2000.

My journaling on this page reads: *"Your first 'ouchie' was a real winner. We were packing the car and planning to leave for New Bern on Memorial Day morning. You were helping Daddy fold the highchair when the middle finger on your left hand got caught. You're such a great baby! You cried a little, but you were fairly calm.… The quick swelling and discoloration made it obvious that you would need medical attention.… We took you to Northcross Medical Center where … an X-ray showed that the tip of your finger had been slightly fractured. … The picture below was taken within 10 minutes of our arrival back home. The pain had subsided and you were proudly showing off your new bandages."*

DESIGN NOTE: To create the tag pocket on this page, I simply folded down the corner of the top piece of cardstock.

"Ouch"

SUPPLIES

Textured cardstock: Bazzill Basics; *Patterned paper:* 7 Gypsies; *Beaded chain:* Making Memories; *Computer fonts:* Copperplate Gothic and Carpenter ICG, downloaded from the Internet; Courier New, Microsoft Word; *Other:* Eyelets.

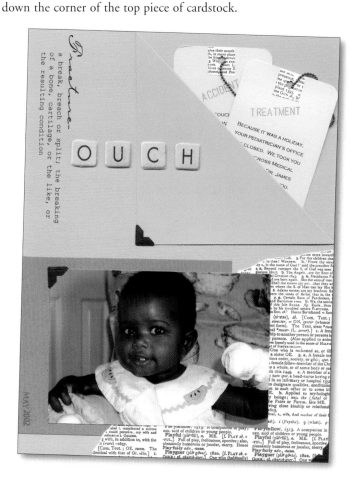

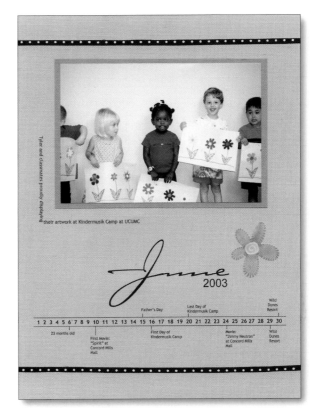

"Kindermusik Camp"

SUPPLIES
Textured cardstock: Bazzill Basics; *Sticker:* Sticko by EK Success; *Computer fonts:* Trebuchet and Carpenter, downloaded from the Internet; Arial, Microsoft Word; *Other:* Ribbon.

Tyler and her classmates proudly display their artwork at Kindermusik Camp at University City United Methodist Church.

On this page, I share the things I'm thankful for in my life by listing several items on tags that read: *A kind husband and a sweet, bright daughter; a mother who loves me unconditionally; a fulfilling career in a creative field; and soundness of mind, body and spirit.* What are you thankful for in your life? Record your blessings on a scrapbook page.

"Gratitude"

SUPPLIES
Patterned paper and stickers: me & my BIG ideas; *Transparency:* Magic Scraps; *Metal letters, jump rings, washer and definition:* Making Memories; *Tags:* 7 Gypsies; *Tag embellishment:* Embellish It; *Jute and string:* The Robin's Nest Press; *Black embroidery floss:* DMC; *Chalk:* EK Success; *Stamping ink:* Stampin' Up!; *Charms:* Above the Mark (mask), source unknown (cross); *Pen:* Zig Writer, EK Success; *Computer font:* Mom's Typewriter, downloaded from the Internet; *Other:* Staples, eyelet tape and metallic paper.

I recorded notes from our family history on this scrapbook page. My mother was asked to share a brief history of her parents at a recent family reunion. Here's an excerpt from the page: *"Papa and Mama made their living as farmers. They provided meat for their family by raising hogs, cattle and chickens. They also had a large vegetable garden. The garden included beans, peas, wheat, corn, okra and tomatoes. Papa would take our wheat to the mill on a horse-drawn wagon."*

"Family History Album"

SUPPLIES

Textured cardstock: Bazzill Basics; *Patterned papers:* Design Originals, Anna Griffin and Karen Foster Design; *Rubber stamps:* Stampers Anonymous, Rubber Baby Buggy Bumpers and Stampin' Up!; *Letter stamps:* Making Memories; *Stamping ink:* Stampin' Up!; Brilliance, Tsukineko; Anna Griffin; *Black letters:* Li'l Davis Designs; *Green stamps:* Collage Joy; *Ruler:* Nostalgiques, EK Success; *Photo corners:* Canson; *Computer font:* Antique Type, downloaded from the Internet; *Label maker:* Dymo; *Self-adhesive fastener:* Acco; *Other:* Manila folder and walnut ink.

"Quote Book"

SUPPLIES

Textured cardstock: Bazzill Basics; *Patterned papers:* 7 Gypsies and L'il Davis Designs; *Silver charm:* Blue Moon; *Beaded chain:* Making Memories; *Computer fonts:* Mom's Typewriter, Antique Type and Graverplate, downloaded from the Internet; *Red pen:* Zig Writer, EK Success; *Library cards and envelopes:* Scraps Ahoy; *Eyelets:* Prym-Dritz; *Stamping ink:* Stampin' Up; *Rubber stamps:* Stampin' Up, Stampers Anonymous, Above the Mark, Anita's and Rubber Stampede; *Other:* Ribbon and leather lacing

In my 12th grade English class, we were required to maintain "Reading Notebooks." What a pain they were! We had to document in a composition book interesting quotes, passages and poems that we'd read. And the most painful part was that we were required to annotate each entry with personal thoughts, questions and insights about each quote.

This exercise, however, launched my life-long love of quotes. I've collected and compiled quotes in various notebooks and journals since my senior year. I decided to compile a few of my favorites in this little album, complete with annotations that HONESTLY describe why each quote is meaningful to me.

An example? The quote: *"Undoubtedly, we become what we envision."*

My journaling: *"I love this quote! But instead of this one, I probably should have included the quote, 'You are what you believe.' Yes, you become what you envision … but what you envision is preceded by some notion or belief."*

how to create your own LIBRARY CARD BOOK

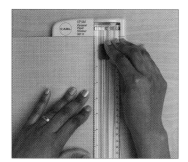

Figure 1

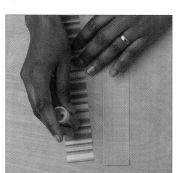

Figure 2

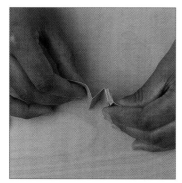

Figure 3

Figure 4

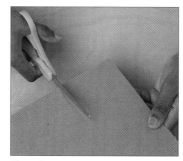

Figure 5

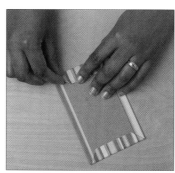

Figure 6

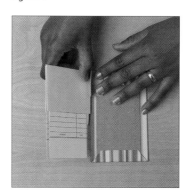

Figure 7

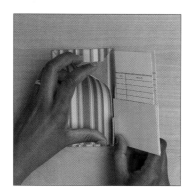

Figure 8

STEP-BY-STEP

1. Cut two 1" x 12" strips of paper. *See Figure 1.*

2. Adhere the two strips together with the wrong sides facing. You can use spray adhesive or a glue stick. *See Figure 2.*

3. Fold the strip accordion style. The folds should be approximately ½" deep. Use a bone folder to crease each fold (the folds will be crisper and the book will lie flatter). *See Figure 3.*

4. Attach a library pocket to the front of each fold. *See Figure 4.*

5. Glue the underside of each fold together.

6. Cut two pieces of chipboard (available at craft and art supply stores) for the front and back covers. *See Figure 5.*

7. Cover the chipboard with decorative paper. *See Figure 6.*

8. Attach the front and back covers to the accordion spine. *See Figure 7.*

9. Cut endpapers slightly smaller than the covers. Attach the endpapers to the inside front and back covers to hide any unfinished covers. *See Figure 8.*

live life
TWO
A week before Tyler's second birthday, George and I began explaining to her that she would soon be two years old. And we taught her how to hold up two fingers instead of one. Well, Tyler decided to put her own spin on her second year milestone. When asked how old she was, Tyler would proudly hold up two fingers on one hand, one finger on the other hand and exclaim "Two months old"!

"Live Life"

SUPPLIES

Textured cardstock: Bazzill Basics; *Patterned papers:* 7 Gypsies and Design Originals; *Word rub-ons, metal letters, frame and ribbon:* Making Memories; *Ruler:* Nostalgiques, EK Success; *Computer font:* Typist, downloaded from the Internet; *Other:* Playing cards.

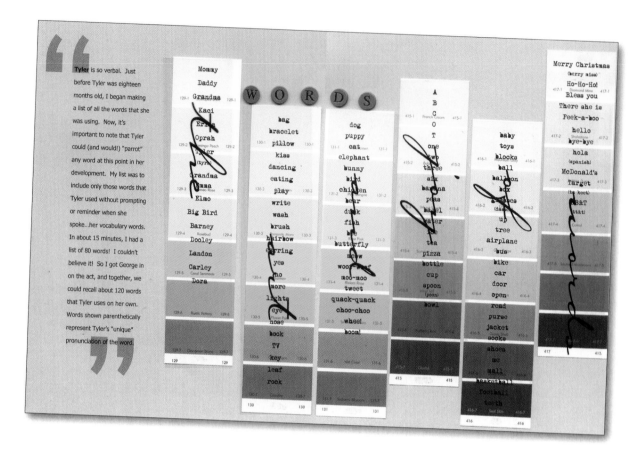

"Tyler's Words"

SUPPLIES

Textured cardstock: Bazzill Basics; *Metal letters:* Making Memories; *Computer fonts:* Century Gothic, Mom's Typewriter and Carpenter ICG, downloaded from the Internet; Tahoma, Microsoft Word; *Other:* Paint chips and transparencies.

My journaling: *"Tyler is so verbal. Just before she turned 18 months old, I began making a list of all the words she was using. Now, it's important to note that Tyler could (and would!) 'parrot' any word at this point in her development. My list included only those words that Tyler used without prompting … her vocabulary words. In about 15 minutes, I had a list of 80 words. I couldn't believe it. So, I got my husband in on the act, and together, we recalled about 120 words Tyler uses on her own."*

On this page, I recorded Tyler's vocabulary words by printing them directly onto paint chips. I created my title, "The Art and Joy of Words," by printing each word on a transparency and then cutting and layering them over the paint chips.

"God Bless America"

SUPPLIES

Textured cardstock: Bazzill Basics; *Patterned papers:* K & Company and 7 Gypsies; *Trading stamps:* Collage Joy; *Silver lock washers:* Hillman; *Postage stamp:* Limited Edition Rubber Stamps; *Date stamp:* Office Depot; *Stamping ink:* Anna Griffin, Colorbök; *Mesh:* The Robin's Nest Press; *Beaded chain:* Making Memories; *Brad:* American Pin & Fastener; *Eyelets:* Creative Imaginations; *Leather and suede accents (on tags):* Tandy Leather Company; *Computer font:* Barcoded, downloaded from the Internet; *Other:* Postage label, eyelet tape and staple.

"Made from Scratch"

SUPPLIES

Textured cardstock: Bazzill Basics; *Patterned paper and twill:* 7 Gypsies; *Ribbon:* C.M. Offray & Son; *Brads:* American Pin & Fastener; *Copper word plate:* Pixie Press; *Computer fonts:* Mom's Typewriter and Top Secret, downloaded from the Internet; *Eyelets:* Prym-Dritz; *Beaded chain:* Making Memories; *Stamping ink:* Stampin' Up!; *Pen:* Zig Writer, EK Success; *Other:* Index cards, jump ring and walnut ink.

We're so lucky to live in America! On this page, I created a tag with the phrase "God Bless America." The "bar code" on the tag is actually a computer font called Barcoded. I also included photographs of the front page of the newspaper with a headline about the invasion of Iraq.

"Play"

SUPPLIES
Textured cardstock: Bazzill Basics; *Computer font:* Typist, downloaded from the Internet; *Date stamp:* Office Depot; *Stamping ink:* Susan Branch (brown); Stampin' Up! (green); Brilliance, Tsukineko (white); *Eyelets:* Doodlebug Design; *Definition:* Making Memories; *Ephemera:* me & my BIG ideas; *Other:* Ribbon, patterned papers and Scrabble tiles.

My husband, George, has proven himself to be quite the playmate for Tyler. One summer morning, I had the following conversation with Tyler (as represented on each tag on my layout):

Tyler: Mommy, where's my daddy?

Me: You know where Daddy is!

Tyler: At work!

Me: That's right! He'll be home this evening.

Tyler: (A very long whine and moan combined) But I wanna PLAY *with him!*

Consider using dialogue and snippets of conversations on your pages to tell the story behind your pictures.

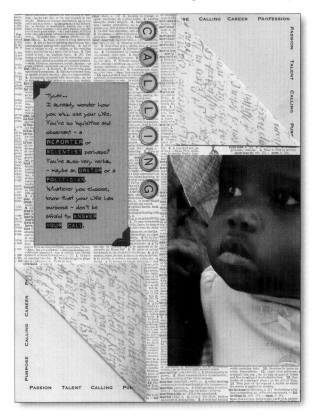

"Answer Your Call"

SUPPLIES
Textured cardstock: Bazzill Basics; *Patterned paper:* Design Originals; *Computer fonts:* Graverplate, Ralph's Hand and Ordner, downloaded from the Internet.

My journaling on this page reads, *"Tyler … I already wonder how you will use your life. You're so inquisitive and observant—a reporter or a scientist, perhaps? You're also very verbal—maybe an orator or a politician. Whatever you choose, know that your life has a purpose— don't be afraid to answer your call."*

Notice the border on my background paper that reads "Passion, Talent, Calling, PURPOSE, Career, Profession."

"Impeccable Manners"

SUPPLIES
Textured cardstock: Bazzill Basics; *Typewriter keys:* 7 Gypsies; *Computer font:* Batik, downloaded from the Internet.

Tyler's grandma says that Tyler is "the most mannerly little girl she's ever met." My husband and I are proud of the fact that Tyler has impeccable manners for a two-year-old. Some of the phrases she uses include: "More please," "Thank you," "I sorry" and "'Scuse me."

"When Did I Become My Mother?"

SUPPLIES
Textured cardstock: Bazzill Basics; *Patterned paper:* Paper Pizazz; *Label maker:* Dymo; *Computer font:* Mom's Typewriter, downloaded from the Internet; *Pen:* Zig Writer, EK Success; *Other:* Masking tape.

When did I become my mother? Sometimes when I hear myself reprimand or warn Tyler, I almost turn to see if my mother is in the room with me. She guided me to make the RIGHT CHOICES, and I do the same with my daughter with phrases I've heard for years: "Please be careful!" "Because I said so!" "Your face will freeze!"

"Ask Mr. Webster"

SUPPLIES
Textured cardstock: Bazzill Basics; *Patterned papers:* 7 Gypsies and Li'l Davis Designs; *Ephemera:* Limited Edition Rubber Stamps and Collage Joy; *Computer fonts:* Arcana Manuscript, Antique Type and Mom's Typewriter, downloaded from the Internet; *Other:* Staples and film.

When I'd ask my mother the definition of a word, she always replied, "Ask Mr. Webster!" I must credit some of my love for words and lettering to her constantly sending me to the dictionary. By the time I was a college freshman, I would actually "read" the dictionary. I received some major abuse from my roommate, who was a senior!

"Crockett Miller Slave Quarters"

SUPPLIES

Textured cardstock: Bazzill Basics; *Patterned papers:* Rusty Pickle, Design Originals and Creative Imaginations; *Ruler:* Nostalgiques, EK Success; *Brads:* Making Memories; *Postage stamps:* Limited Edition Rubber Stamps; *Rubber stamps:* Stampers Anonymous and Rubber Baby Buggy Bumpers; *Stamping ink:* Brilliance, Tsukineko; *Keyhole:* Li'l Davis Designs; *Ephemera:* Collage Joy and me & my BIG ideas; *Computer font:* Mom's Typewriter, downloaded from the Internet; *Other:* Square clip, hinges and staple.

My husband's hometown, New Bern, North Carolina, has an amazingly rich history. It was one of the country's first settlements for freed slaves. Grandma Emma sent Tyler the attached note and article about the preservation of former slave quarters in New Bern to share the history.

To create this layout, I hinged two pieces of cardstock together to create the look of a book. The inside of the left-hand page includes the actual note written to Tyler from her grandmother. The right-hand page includes a photocopy of the article.

"Holiday Memories 2002"

SUPPLIES
Textured cardstock: Bazzill Basics; *Patterned papers:* Frances Meyer and Paper Pizazz; *Buttons:* Dress It Up; *Computer fonts:* Scriptina and Arcana, downloaded from the Internet; Tahoma, Microsoft Word.

For my journaling on this page, I listed our holiday memories from Christmas in 2002. I used buttons as bullet points to highlight each special memory. Consider using eyelets, brads, stickers or buttons to create a similar page detailing your family traditions (during the holidays or anytime of the year).

We had several very cold and rainy days during the month of October. Instead of playing outside, I decided Tyler should begin learning the alphabet. I printed the letter "A" for her in a large font. She started saying the letter "A," and within a few days, I could point to an "A" in print and she would identify it. I was so proud when we were shopping at Wal-Mart one day and she started saying "A, A, A!" She'd spotted the "A's" in the word "Wal-Mart" on the seat buckle of the shopping cart.

To create this page, I used patterned paper and corkboard to reinforce the school theme. Think about the importance of education in your life. What lessons have you taught and learned that show how you value the importance of learning?

"Tyler's First Letter"

SUPPLIES
Textured cardstock: Bazzill Basics; *Patterned papers and metal letters:* Making Memories; *Cork:* Magic Scraps; *Brads:* American Pin & Fastener; *Flower accent:* Jolee's by You, Sticko by EK Success; *Pens:* Zig Writers, EK Success; *Computer fonts:* Garamouche, downloaded from the Internet; Arial, Microsoft Word; *Ribbon:* C.M. Offray & Son; *Other:* Jute and Mother Goose image.

Tolerance · Traditions

Holiday Memories 2002

- Visiting The Naughtons in Ballantyne
- Exchanging gifts with The Wiggins at our house
- Eating Christmas Eve dinner at Grandma Morrow's house with Aunt Debbie and her family
- Opening my Santa gifts on Christmas Eve
- Spending Christmas morning with Aunt Pansy and her family in Clayton
- Sharing Christmas Day dinner with family at Grandma Emma's house
- Meeting Uncle Shelf for the first time
- Visiting Aunt Mable in the nursing home
- Attending the Blessing Ceremony for Aunt Sharon and Uncle Napoleon

Trust · Unity · Vision

I love to read! I'm always finding inspiration in books and magazines. Here are a few of my favorites titles:

Faye's Favorites

MAGAZINES

In Style
www.InStyle.com

Mary Engelbreit's Home Companion
www.maryengelbreit.com

O, The Oprah Magazine
www.oprah.com

Veranda
www.veranda.com

BOOKS

Creating a Beautiful Home
Alexandra Stoddard

Designing Women
Margaret Russell

Living a Beautiful Life
Alexandra Stoddard

A Room of Her Own
Chris Casson Madden

Simple Abundance
Sara Ban Breathnach

from the
HOME
— of —
Faye Morrow Bell

... marathon phone conversations ... seeing Kate Spade together in person ... supporting each other through potty training. There is no substitute for the 27-year friendship I've had with my best friend Pansy. Aristotle said, "Wishing to be friends is quick work, but friendship is a slow ripening fruit." Few things are as sweet as a cherished friend.

Faye

Family history is important to us. So important, in fact, that we've incorporated family surnames into our living room décor. We can hardly wait to begin sharing our legacy with Tyler. As John Steinbeck said, "How will our children know who they are if they don't know where they come from?"

dining room
wallpaper

photography S.O.S.

"Language of Friendship"

SUPPLIES

Textured cardstock: Bazzill Basics;
Rubber stamp: Inkadinkadoo; *Stamping
ink:* Anna Griffin; *Compass:* Manto Fev;
Dog tag: Chronicle Books; *Screen wire:*
Elgar Products; *Ephemera:* Stampa
Rosa; *Brad:* American Pin & Fastener;
Computer fonts: Donny's Hand, Texas
Hero, Graverplate and Amphion, down-
loaded from the Internet; *Other:* Index
prints and paint chip.

My best friend, Pansy, and I are huge Kate Spade fans. We were thrilled to hear that she was making an appearance in Charlotte to debut her new fragrance, Kate Spade Beauty. We were so pleased to be among the fans who got to meet her as she autographed purses and bottles of fragrance.

We didn't have any great close-ups of Kate, and the pictures were a bit on the dark side. Instead of trimming the photos into tiny rectangles, I decided to use a template and cut windows in my scrapbook page. By using light cardstock and slipping the photos behind the windows, I emphasized the portions of the pictures showing Kate signing autographs.

This is a great technique to use for photographs that were taken from a distance or in a place with poor lighting. School programs, dance recitals and baseball games are just a few occasions where you may end up with similar photographs. Using light colors and a clean design will ensure your pictures remain the highlight of your page.

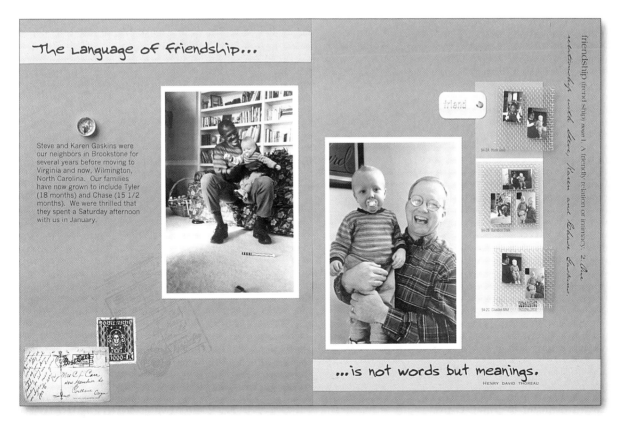

The Language of friendship...

Steve and Karen Gaskins were our neighbors in Brookstone for several years before moving to Virginia and now, Wilmington, North Carolina. Our families have now grown to include Tyler (18 months) and Chase (15 1/2 months). We were thrilled that they spent a Saturday afternoon with us in January.

friend

...is not words but meanings.
HENRY DAVID THOREAU

photo-transfer technique with PACKING TAPE

Looking for an unusual way to create a birth announcement? When my friend, Donna Downey's, son was born, I thought it would be fun to create a keepsake that incorporated several different types of media, including a white canvas background, a paint chip with enticing paint names such as "Charm Blue" and "Lake of Lucerne," silk ribbons and a mock-soda cap lid.

"Cole Patrick"

SUPPLIES
Pen: Zig Writer, EK Success; *Letter stickers (bottle caps):* Li'l Davis Designs; *Canvas board:* Royal and Langnickel; *Other:* Packing tape, paint chip and ribbon.

Step 1

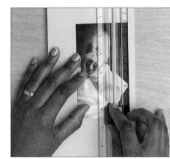

Step 2

Step 3

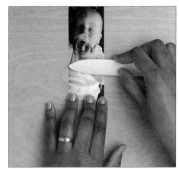

Step 4

Step 5

Step 6

STEP-BY-STEP To create this keepsake, I started by transferring the picture of Cole to a piece of packing tape. Here are the simple steps I followed:

1. I chose a photograph of Cole and made a copy of it. You can use a black-and-white copy or a color copy.

2. I cut the copy so it would fit on a strip of packing tape.

3. I attached the copy to the sticky side of the tape.

4. Using a bone folder, I burnished the image onto the tape by repeatedly rubbing the stick over the non-sticky side of the tape. (You could also use a Popsicle stick or a spoon.)

5. I placed the burnished image into a tub of very warm water.

6. After several minutes, I took the image out of the water and rubbed off the paper from my photocopy. The result? The image of Cole transferred to a piece of clear packing tape, which I then layered over the paint chip and canvas board on my design.

This packing-tape transfer also works well with magazine advertisements. Try layering several images on your packing tape to create a collage effect.

A MINI-DESIGN CHALLENGE: It's fun to see how you can combine an assortment of unlike items to make a creative card or page accent. The next time you're cropping with your friends, ask everyone to bring an extra set of supplies they rarely use. Put the supplies into groups and ask everyone to create a card, tag or page accent with the materials they're given. Another idea? Challenge yourself to combine unlike textures—canvas and silk, metal rivets and lace, cardboard and cotton—and see what you can create.

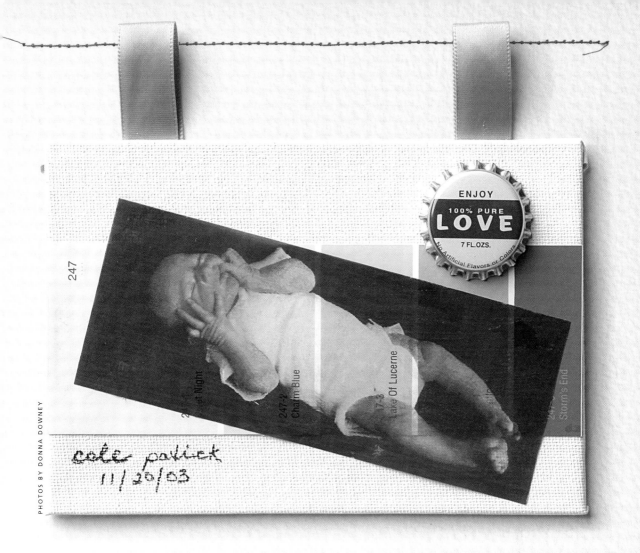

PHOTOS BY DONNA DOWNEY

cole patrick
11/20/03

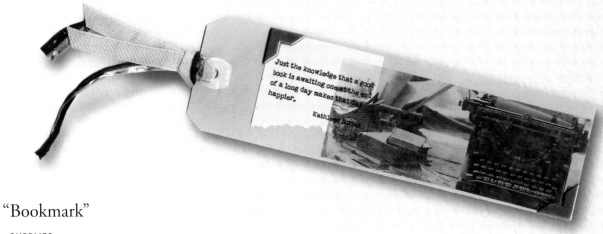

Just the knowledge that a good book is awaiting one at the end of a long day makes that day happier.

Kathleen Norris

"Bookmark"

SUPPLIES
Patterned paper: Anna Griffin; *Fibers:*
Adornaments, EK Success; *Metal corners:*
Making Memories; *Computer font:*
Underwood No. 5, downloaded from
the Internet, *Other:* Packing tape.

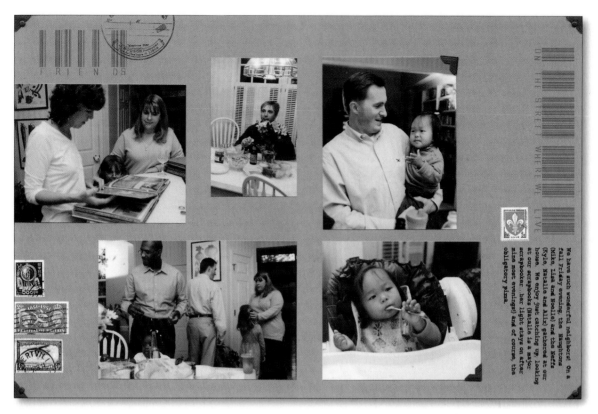

"Friends—On the Street Where We Live"

SUPPLIES
Textured cardstock: Bazzill Basics; *Rubber stamps:* Rubber Baby Buggy Bumpers; *Stamping ink:* StazOn, Tsukineko; *Date stamp:* Office Depot; *Postage stamps:* Limited Edition Rubber Stamps; *Photo corners:* Canson; *Brads:* Doodlebug Design; *Computer fonts:* Barcoding, downloaded from the Internet; CK Typewriter, "Fresh Fonts" CD, *Creating Keepsakes.*

"Keepsake Gift Bag"

SUPPLIES
Patterned paper: DMD, Inc.; *Fabric paper and medallion:* K & Company; *Twill:* 7 Gypsies; *Bookplate:* Li'l Davis Designs; *Brads:* Doodlebug Design; *Other:* Cover from an old book.

"Miss You" Card

SUPPLIES
Twill tape: Creek Bank; *Blue paint:* Plaid; *Rubber stamps:* Limited Edition Rubber Stamps (eyes) and Stampers Anonymous (clock); *Stamping ink:* StazOn (black), Tsukineko; *Stampin' Up!* (white); *Letter stamps:* Making Memories; *Other:* Reflectors from auto parts store and brads.

"Cheerios"

SUPPLIES
Textured cardstock: Bazill Basics; *Computer fonts:* Times New Roman, Microsoft Word; Xerox Sans Serif, downloaded from the Internet; *Label maker:* Dymo; *Eyelets:* Doodlebug Design.

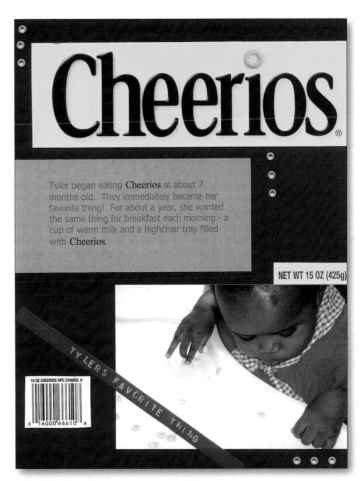

Tyler began eating **Cheerios** at about 7 months old. They immediately became her favorite thing! For about a year, she wanted the same thing for breakfast each morning - a cup of warm milk and a highchair tray filled with **Cheerios**.

NET WT 15 OZ (425g)

TYLER'S FAVORITE THING

marine corps marathon MINI-BOOK

When my friend, Debbie Smith, ran her first marathon (the Marine Corps marathon), I wanted to create a special album to celebrate her accomplishment. I created this six-page mini-album, made from graduated pieces of cardstock (the last page is 11" long, the next to last page is 10½" long, and so on) that are attached with a prong fastener. I divided the album into sections labeled "Marathon," "Faithful," "Debbie," "Shoes" and "Medal," and included the marathon emblem on the front cover of the album.

Mini-albums are wonderful gifts to share with friends and loved ones. Choose a special event to highlight, celebrate the facets of your friendship, or add a mini-album to a scrapbook page to increase the number of photographs displayed. Another idea? Give mini-albums as "thank you" gifts for teachers or other special people in your life. Fill them with photographs, quotes, inspirational stories, shared adventures and more.

"Marine Corps Book"

SUPPLIES

Textured cardstock: Bazzill Basics; *Ribbon, beaded chain and brads:* Making Memories; *Label maker:* Dymo; *Charm:* Watch Us; *Rubber stamp:* Stampers Anonymous; *Stamping ink:* Stampin' Up!; *Pen:* Zig Writer, EK Success; *Computer fonts:* Tablhoide, Texas Hero, Mom's Typewriter and Top Secret, downloaded from the Internet; *Other:* Prong fastener, chalk and patch from marathon.

STEP-BY-STEP You can create a gift album or an interactive layout simply by using easily accessible supplies such as cardstock and a prong fastener (available at office supply stores). To make your own mini-album, follow these simple steps:

1. Cut cardstock in varying lengths. On my Marine Corps marathon book, I cut each sheet ½" longer than the previous one.

2. Using your prong fastener as a template, mark where you will want to punch your holes.

3. Punch holes through all layers of the cardstock.

4. Insert prong fastener.

5. Decorate as desired.

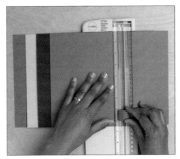

Step 1

Step 2

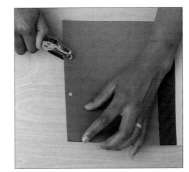

Step 3

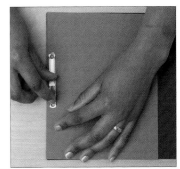

Step 4

"Grandma Emma and Aunt Sharon"

SUPPLIES

Textured cardstock: Bazzill Basics; *Patterned papers:* Frances Meyers (red) 7 Gypsies (brown), Source unknown (gingham); *Photo turns and twill:* 7 Gypsies; *Brads:* Doodlebug Design and American Pin & Fastener; *Bookplate:* L'il Davis Design; *Staples:* Making Memories; *Heart charm:* Watch Us; *Tag:* me & my BIG idea; *Fresh cuts:* EK Success; *Other:* Dymo labeler.

BABY CARD book

When Tyler was born, my husband and I received cards and notes from friends and family congratulating us on our brand-new daughter. I wanted to preserve all the well wishes, so I decided to make a "card book." I covered chipboard with fabric-inspired paper and added pictures of baby Tyler to the front cover. To complete this simple book, I punched holes in the upper left of the items and fastened them with a beaded chain.

VARIATION This idea can easily be adapted to holiday, birthday and anniversary cards. Alter an old deck of cards with the miniature pictures your child brings home from school after picture day. Include photos of your child and her best friends, and caption each card like a baseball card, with titles, "stats" and achievements. Punch holes in the upper-left-hand corner of each card and loop them together with a key chain or metal ring. This non-traditional "yearbook" will be a fun way for your child to remember her classmates from year to year.

"Baby Card Book"

SUPPLIES

Textured cardstock: Bazzill Basics; *Patterned paper:* Making Memories; *Twill:* 7 Gypsies; *Bookplates:* Li'l Davis Designs; *Brads:* Doodlebug Design; *Beaded chain and ribbon:* Making Memories; *Rivet:* Chatterbox; *Charm:* Card Connection.

SLIDE page layout

"Thanksgiving Day with Neighbors"

SUPPLIES

Textured cardstock: Bazzill Basics; *Circle tag:* Hillman; *Square punch:* Marvy Uchida; *Chinese coin:* World Market; *Brads:* American Pin & Fastener; *Chalks:* Craf-T Products; *Pen:* Zig Writer, EK Success; *Computer fonts:* Texas Hero, Ordner and Batik, downloaded from the Internet; 2Peas Cookie Dough, downloaded from *www.twopeasinabucket.com; Other:* Plastic slide page, film, picture hanger, ribbon, beads, fiber and raffia.

My family and I are lucky to be blessed with such special neighbors. Dinner and coffee with our neighbors indeed made for the perfect ending to Thanksgiving Day in 2002. To create this layout, I used a slide page to hold each layout element. Note that the three "tabs" on the right side ("Coffee," "Dessert" and "Friends") summarize the event. I tore and chalked the title, then attached it to a metal picture hanger.

The quote on the right side of the layout reads: *"For health and food, for love of friends, for everything thy goodness sends, Father in Heaven, we thank thee."*

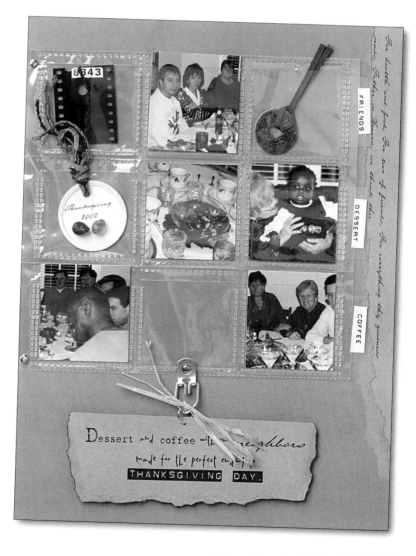

HIDDEN journaling

This special layout celebrates an exciting time in our friends' lives. The tag pulls out to reveal this journaling: *"We could not be any more excited for our dear friends, Mike and Lisa Naughton! After what seemed like an eternal adoption process, Mike and Lisa traveled to China in March 2003 to bring home their darling 11-month-old daughter, Noelle. This picture was taken on the day we first met Noelle."*

I created the title of this page ("Family") with a computer font and a rub-on text transfer. Look for opportunities to combine fonts (computer fonts, rubber stamps, text patterned paper, sticker phrases, rub-ons and more) to create attractive graphic elements for your pages.

"Family—Happily Ever After"

SUPPLIES

Textured cardstock: Bazzill Basics; *Patterned papers:* Rusty Pickle, Karen Foster Design and Design Originals; *Fern punch:* The Punch Bunch; *Postage stamps:* Limited Edition Rubber Stamps; *Tag:* Memory Lane Paper Company; *Tassel:* The Trim Shop; *Rubber stamp:* Stampin' Up!; *Stamping ink:* Brilliance, Tsukineko; *Word rub-ons:* Making Memories; *Computer font:* Mom's Typewriter, downloaded from the Internet; *Other:* Chinese coin and bamboo clip.

journaling with your child's words

"What's Up, Doc"

SUPPLIES

Textured cardstock: Bazzill Basics; *Patterned paper, bottle cap, red letters and beaded chain:* Li'l Davis Designs; *Photo turns:* 7 Gypsies; *Trading stamps:* Collage Joy; *Ribbon:* Making Memories; *Eyelet:* Creative Imaginations; *Red embroidery floss:* DMC; *Date stamp:* Office Depot; *Stamping ink:* Anna Griffin; *Computer fonts:* MA Sexy and Mom's Typewriter, downloaded from the Internet; *Other:* Slide holder.

As you'll notice in this chapter, I've included pages that celebrate Tyler's "friendships" with her stuffed animals and toys. One of Tyler's favorite things to do is take care of her stuffed animals. I love hearing Tyler talk to and about her stuffed animals—and I've found that adding Tyler's words to my scrapbook pages makes my journaling that much more meaningful.

My journaling on this layout reads: *"Hardly a day passes that Tyler doesn't mention going to the doctor or the hospital! In February 2003, Tyler and I took Grandma Z home from the hospital when she was discharged after her ankle surgery. Tyler has been fascinated with hospitals and doctors since. Whenever she gets the slightest bump or scrape, she'll say, 'I need to go to Mommy Z's hospital.'"*

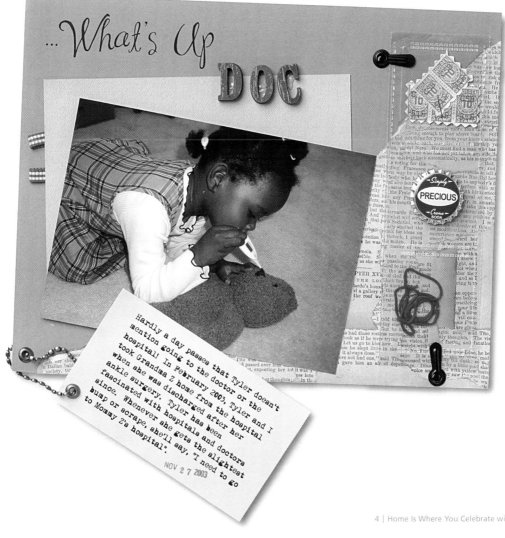

RUBBER STAMPING on your pages

I love stamping on my pages because it's so versatile (you'll find a list of my favorite rubber stamp companies and products in "Faye's Favorites" at the end of this chapter). Throughout this book, you'll see how I've used a variety of rubber stamps to create stamped backgrounds that help tell the story behind my photographs. In this chapter, I share four special techniques you can use on your pages.

FRAME/PHOTO CORNER STAMPS To create the oversized photo corners on this page, I simply inked a frame stamp with black ink and stamped it on taupe cardstock. With a pair of scissors, I cut the frame into corners, which I then embellished with a bit of fiber, metal clips and nametags. To add dimension to my layout, I used pop dots under each corner.

"Let's Scrapbook This Morning"

SUPPLIES
Textured cardstock: Bazzill Basics; *Rubber stamp:* Stampers Anonymous; *Stamping ink:* Brilliance, Tsukineko; Anna Griffin; *Fiber:* The Robin's Nest Press; *Charm:* QVC; *Paper clips:* Making Memories; *Computer fonts:* Top Secret, Mom's Typewriter and Texas Hero, downloaded from the Internet.

"Magazines"

SUPPLIES

Textured cardstock: Bazzill Basics;
Patterned papers: Paper Loft and
7 Gypsies; *Rubber stamp:* Stampers
Anonymous; *Stamping ink:* Stampin'
Up!; *Brads:* Doodlebug Design; *Pen:*
Zig Writer, EK Success; *Computer
fonts:* Ordner and P22 Vincent,
downloaded from the Internet;
Other: Magazine cover.

WORD BLOCK STAMPS My best friend, Pansy, and I just love magazines. In fact, magazines are one of the common bonds that has tied our friend-ship together ever since the 7th grade. We've progressed from *Seventeen, Glamour* and *Victoria* to *O, The Oprah Magazine, Martha Stewart Living* and *Creating Keepsakes.*

To create the white-on-black text featured on this layout, I inked a large word stamp with white ink and stamped it on black cardstock. I used a pair of scissors to cut the image into pieces and attached the different sections to my page. Note how the text becomes a graphic design element that enhances (and doesn't compete with) the text on the magazine cover, my computer fonts and the text on the printed paper.

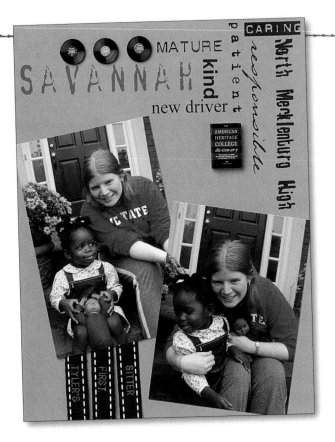

"Savannah"

SUPPLIES
Textured cardstock: Bazzill Basics; *Miniatures:* Small Town Treasures and Joshua's; *Letter stamps:* Cosco; *Stamping ink:* Stampin' Up!; *Computer fonts:* Top Secret, Mom's Typewriter, Ordner, Plastique, Texas Hero and Tablhoide, downloaded from the Internet; Arial and Times New Roman, Microsoft Word; *Other:* Ribbon.

ALPHABET/TEXT STAMPS When I created this layout featuring Tyler and her first babysitter, Savannah, I wanted to include elements that gave the page a "teenage" feel. I stamped the words "Tyler's First Sitter" on black stitched ribbon and aligned the ribbons in a three-part vertical border toward the bottom of the left-hand side of the page.

TEMPLATES AND STAMPS Another quick and easy trick with your stamps, templates and punches? You can take a favorite punch (a circle, a square, even a shaped design), punch the shape from cardstock, ink a stamp, and stamp directly through the punched shape. (See Figure 1.) This easy trick will allow you to change the look of your rubber stamps. (See Figure 2.)

Figure 1

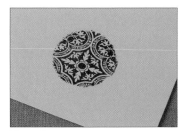

Figure 2

Jaje's Favorites

Here's a list of my favorite rubber stamp and stamping supply companies:

RUBBER STAMPS

Above the Mark
www.abovethemark.com

Rubber Baby Buggy Bumpers
www.rubberbaby.com

River City Rubber Works
www.rivercityrubberworks.com

Stamper's Anonymous
www.stampersanonymous.com

RUBBER STAMPING INKS

Brilliance by Tsukineko
(Graphite Black and Moonlight White)
www.tsukineko.com

Stampin' Up!
(Close to Cocoa)
www.stampinup.com

Susan Branch
(Light Brown)
www.susanbranch.com

VersaMark by Tsukineko
(Watermark Stamp Pad)
www.tsukineko.com

"Easter Sunday"

SUPPLIES
Textured cardstock: Bazzill Basics; *Sticker:* The Okie-Dokie Press; *Label maker:* Dymo; *Bookplate:* 7 Gypsies; *Brads:* Making Memories; *Number rub-ons:* Chartpak; *Computer fonts:* Ordner, Boston, Mom's Typewriter and Stacy's Hand, downloaded from the Internet.

APRIL 20

EASTER SUNDAY 2003

We began our Easter Sunday celebration with Tyler opening her gifts. She received a large Easter basket from Grandma Emma and Aunt Sharon. The basket included bunny ears (see below), white gloves with a matching headband, stacking bunnies, a bunny sippy cup and much, much more! Grandma Emma also sent Tyler several spring outfits. Cousin Mable gave Tyler a sweet Ducky basket with a little stuffed chick inside. We spent the afternoon at Grandma Morrow's house.

We also visited with Aunt Dorothy. Bert and Rodney stopped by while at Aunt Dorothy's house. And then, we returned home to an egg hunt *(see sidebar)*.

THE EGG HUNT

As George and Tyler and I were leaving for my Mother's house, we noticed an Easter Egg in one of our hedges. We knew that our wonderful neighbors, Rex and Robin had placed it there for Tyler to find. When we returned home just before dusk, we then noticed that there were eggs everywhere! George rang the doorbell so that Rex and Robin could join us as Tyler found the dozen hidden eggs. What fun! And Robin had placed goldfish crackers in each egg as she knows that Tyler does not eat candy. What a perfect ending to an Easter day.

1·2

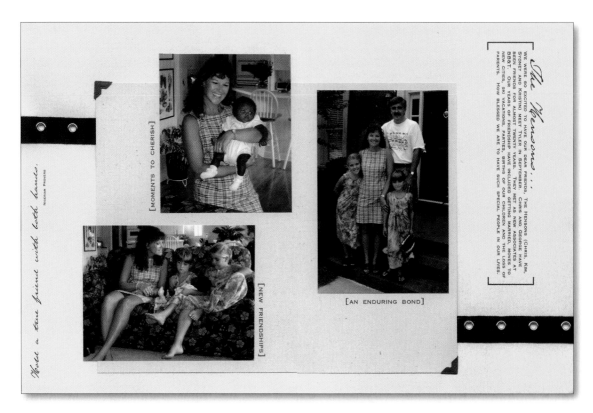

"The Hensons"

SUPPLIES
Textured cardstock: Bazzill Basics; *Photo corners:* Canson; *Computer fonts:* Texas Hero and Graverplate, downloaded from the Internet; *Other:* Eyelet tape.

"Cherish Fond Memories"

SUPPLIES
Textured cardstock: Bazzill Basics; *Patterned paper and photo turns:* 7 Gypsies; *Staples, jump rings and word rub-ons:* Making Memories; *Brads:* Doodlebug Design (copper), Creative Impressions (fleur-de-lis); *Computer fonts:* Top Secret, Inkburrow, Mom's Typewriter and Carlisle, downloaded from the Internet; Arial, Microsoft Word.

"Art"

SUPPLIES
Textured cardstock: Bazzill Basics; *Metal letters:* Making Memories; *Wire:* Amaco; *Computer font:* Times New Roman, Microsoft Word; *Other:* Pencils, envelope, bookplate and jump rings.

We had a wonderful visit with our friends John, Ellen, Johnny and Christie Davis at Emerald Isle in coastal North Carolina. Johnny is quite the artist! 11-month-old Tyler was entertained and amazed at Johnny's abilities with pencils and crayons! And then came Tyler's favorite part of the afternoon. Johnny taught her to "fetch." He would roll (and sometimes throw) tennis balls across the great room of the beach house. Tyler never tired of retrieving them for him!

May 2002

with all my heart...

Landon was Tyler's first doll. I never encouraged her to play with dolls, but she began showing a natural "maternal" interest in them at around nine months old. Whenever we strolled the toy aisles and she spotted a doll that she liked, Tyler would point and excitedly exclaim, "Oh-oh-oh!" So we bought Landon for Tyler just before your first birthday and it's been love ever since! The older Tyler gets, the more she nurtures Landon. She's progressed from just rocking and hugging and kissing him to teaching him! Tyler reads books to Landon and she's taught him Itsy Bitsy Spider. One of Tyler's favorite activities is to take Landon to the foyer transoms and point out passing walkers and hikers! You can also see from the photographs that Tyler enjoys changing Landon's clothes.

Rock-a-bye

BABY

LUV

bottles ROCKING singing
[ʌʊ][ʌʊ] talking hugging
changing diapers watching TV
clapping hands riding in the stroller
reading HAND GAMES feeding

KISSES

"Baby Luv"

SUPPLIES

Textured cardstock: Bazzill Basics; *Ribbon:* C.M. Offray & Son; *Metal letters:* Making Memories; *Acrylic paint:* Plaid; *Computer fonts:* Garamouche, Texas Hero, Graverplate, Ordner, Paper Cuts, Ticket Capitals, Batik, Ralph's Hand, Quest's Hand and P22 Vincent, downloaded from the Internet; Arial, Microsoft Word; 2Peas Ribbon and 2Peas Cookie Dough, down-loaded from *www.twopeasinabucket.com;* *Other:* Safety pins and staples.

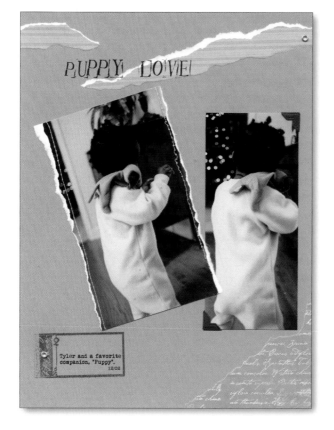

PUPPY LOVE

Tyler and a favorite companion, "Puppy". 12/02

"Puppy Love"

SUPPLIES

Textured cardstock: Bazzill Basics; *Vellum:* The Write Stock; *Eyelet:* Doodlebug Design; *Rubber stamps:* Stampin' Up! and Inkadinkadoo; *Stamping ink:* Stampin' Up!; *Computer fonts:* Mom's Typewriter and Ticket Capitals, downloaded from the Internet; *Other:* Patterned paper.

I'm often asked how I developed my artistic style. Just like everyone, I have my favorite scrapbooking tools and forms of media I like to use over and over again. The formula for my look includes rubber stamps, some patterned text paper, a couple of fonts and a black-and-white photograph for good measure. The following supplies are some of my favorites:

RUBBER STAMPS I love rubber stamps for their versatility and the dimension they add to my work. My favorite rubber stamps are ones with text and circular elements. Because so many of the lines and embellishments in scrapbooking are straight, rubber stamps with circular elements add movement to my work.

PATTERNED TEXT PAPER I've always been intrigued with words and lettering. I literally have a collection of patterned text paper! Most patterned text papers are printed in neutral shades with a classic look that fits perfectly with my artistic style.

BAZZILL BASICS CARDSTOCK I rarely use cardstock other than Bazzill Basics. I love the weight and feel of their papers. Their range of colors is amazing, and they have some of the best shades of green.

METAL ACCENTS I favor cool color palettes. Silver metals are the perfect enhancement for my work.

TWILL AND RIBBON My fondness for ribbon and twill is connected to my first hobby, sewing. There's something very natural to me about incorporating sewing notions, especially ribbon and twill, into my work.

COMPUTER FONTS I'm intrigued by the art of typography, and incorporating computer fonts into my work is a great way for me to explore this interest. With PowerPoint software and the incredible array of fonts available, it's easy for the text to become a graphical element in my artwork as well.

BLACK-AND-WHITE PHOTOGRAPHS Black-and-white photography is very honest. Black-and-white photographs pull me in and engage me in a way color can't.

Think of how you get "your look" on scrapbook pages. What types of supplies do you reach for on a regular basis? Try putting your favorites into categories, and I'll bet you'll notice your own personal style emerging.

from the
HOME
— of —
Faye Morrow Bell

my studio

Author Sara Ban Breathnach reminds
us that everyday life should be a
celebration. I celebrate long walks on
the greenway with George and Tyler...
fresh flowers for my studio...cooking
shrimp and grits for dinner... coloring
with Tyler...reading in my club chair...
the morning phone call from my mother...
discovering a new issue of a favorite
magazine. I celebrate who I am.
I celebrate who I am becoming.

Faye

There's no substitute for a place to
call your own—that place where you
leave more centered and alive than when
you arrived. Maybe that place is your
favorite reading chair, your flower
garden or the nook you've claimed in
your bedroom. I find sanctuary in my
studio. There's nothing like the feeling
of becoming completely absorbed and
immersed in my art.

PAINT CHIP layout

I was riding the escalator in a major airport when I looked up to see huge, colorful flags hanging from the ceiling. The flags were arranged in an interesting geometric pattern. Their arrangement combined with the profusion of color reminded me of a bouquet of flowers. I've never forgotten that image; it inspired me to create a "bouquet" of paint chips.

STEP-BY-STEP Here's how to re-create it:

1. Obtain 12 paint chips of various colors.

2. Trim each paint chip to 1½" x 5".

3. Cut a 6" x 11" cardstock base.

4. Accordion-fold the cardstock. The folds should be approximately 1⅜" wide.

5. Adhere the paint chips to the folded cardstock. Place two paint chips on each fold. The front faces of the paint chips should alternate directions.

6. Add an eyelet and beaded chain to one end of the cardstock base.

7. Adhere the remaining end of the cardstock base to your layout.

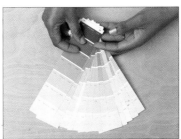

Step 1

Step 2

Step 3

Step 5

Step 4

Step 6

a tribute to PATTERNED TEXT PAPER

I'll admit it. I have a huge weakness for patterned paper with text on it. Although I buy tons of scrapbooking supplies, I'm reasonable about buying things that complement my style and that I know I'll use. Well, that rationale goes completely out the window when it comes to patterned text paper. And it really doesn't help that most papers with text are in neutral colors like cream, brown and black. I can always justify buying a sheet, knowing I can easily incorporate it "somewhere." I present my "Homage to Patterned Paper" on this interactive scrapbook page. Note how I displayed patterned paper in a variety of ways, including on several tag shapes and inside metal frames.

TIP: I used lightweight, scalloped hinges to attach the top layer of my layout. You can find these hinges in the dollhouse or woodcrafts sections at craft supply stores like Michaels.

What do you collect? Consider creating a scrapbook page that reflects your collections. Journal about the appeal of the items, the reason you started your collection and so on.

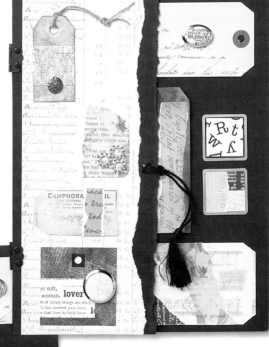

"Tribute to Patterned Text Paper"

SUPPLIES
Textured cardstock: Bazzill Basics; *Patterned papers:* 7 Gypsies, Rusty Pickle, Design Originals and Paper Pizazz; *Globe:* Scraps Ahoy; *Conchos:* Scrapworks; *Tags:* DMD, Inc. and Making Memories; *Brads:* American Pin & Fastener; *Watch face:* 7 Gypsies; *Other:* Jute, lock washers, walnut ink and tassel.

"It's Lisa Bearnson"

SUPPLIES
Textured cardstock: Bazzill Basics;
Computer fonts: Plastique and Ralph's
Hand, downloaded from the Internet;
Tahoma, Microsoft Word.

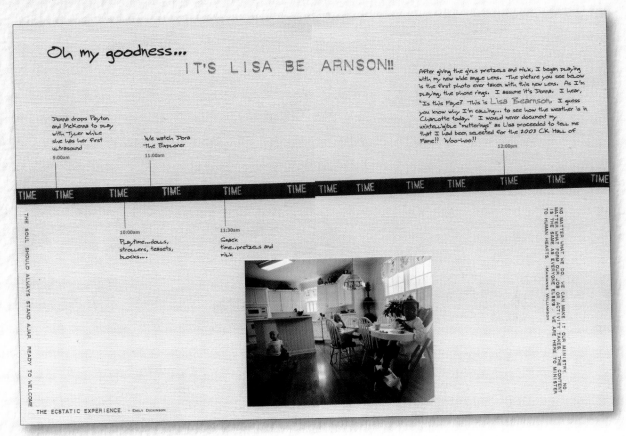

Oh my goodness...
IT'S LISA BE ARNSON!!

After giving the girls pretzels and milk, I began playing with my new wide angle lens. The picture you see below is the first photo ever taken with this new lens. As I'm playing, the phone rings. I assume it's Donna. I hear, "Is this Faye? This is Lisa Bearnson. I guess you know why I'm calling... to see how the weather is in Charlotte today." I would never document my unintelligible "mutterings" as Lisa proceeded to tell me that I had been selected for the 2003 CK Hall of Fame!! Woo-hoo!!

Donna drops Payton and McKenna to play with Tyler while she has her first ultrasound
9:00am

We watch Dora The Explorer
11:00am

12:00pm

TIME TIME TIME TIME TIME TIME TIME TIME TIME TIME TIME TIME TIME

10:00am
Playtime...dolls, strollers, teasets, blocks.....

11:30am
Snack time..pretzels and milk

THE SOUL SHOULD ALWAYS STAND AJAR, READY TO WELCOME THE ECSTATIC EXPERIENCE. - EMILY DICKINSON

NO MATTER WHAT WE DO, WE CAN MAKE IT OUR MINISTRY. NO MATTER WHAT FORM OUR JOB OR ACTIVITY TAKES, THE CONTENT IS THE SAME AS EVERYONE ELSE'S: WE ARE HERE TO MINISTER TO HUMAN HEARTS. -MARIANNE WILLIAMSON

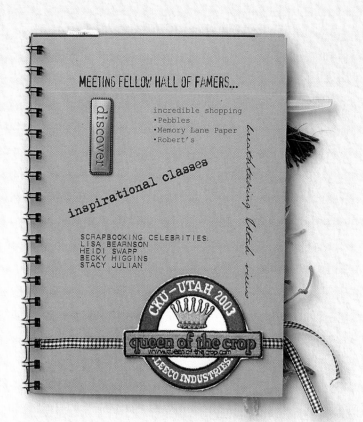

"CKU-Utah"

SUPPLIES

Textured cardstock: Bazzill Basics; *Beaded chain, black tag, eyelets and metal letters:* Making Memories; *"Discover" plaque:* Li'l Davis Designs; *"Queen of the Crop" badge:* Leeco Industries; *Red wired fiber and gold ribbon:* The Robin's Nest Press; *Computer fonts:* Top Secret, Plastique, Mom's Typewriter and Texas Hero, downloaded from the Internet; Courier New, Microsoft Word; *Ribbon:* C.M. Offray & Son; *Other:* CKU ticket stubs, ribbons and fibers.

creating keepsakes university (CKU) BOOK

STEP-BY-STEP You can easily create your own cardstock book. Here's how:

1. Cut a front and back cover (8½" x 10½") from cardstock.

2. Score the front and back covers at 4¼".

3. Fold the covers and burnish with a bone folder.

4. Decorate the covers as desired.

5. Cut several sheets of cardstock to make your inside pages. My pages measure 8½" x 5½".

6. Decorate the inside pages.

7. Bring the covers and pages to a copy store and ask them to bind your book for you.

CKU-Utah 2003 was my first CKU experience. What an amazing time I had. It's hard to explain the energy that emanates from 600 women who are as passionate about scrapbooking as I am! To preserve my special memories of CKU, I made a book from cardstock, added photographs and inserted my class tickets inside the book.

When you scrapbook important events, consider adding items such as movie tickets, brochures, postcards, programs, class schedules and more to your layouts. Including these "extras" helps tell a more complete story.

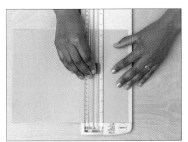

Step 1

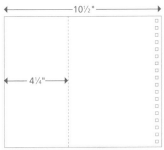

Step 2

Step 3

"Quiet"

SUPPLIES
Textured cardstock: Bazzill Basics; *Patterned papers:* Anna Griffin and Scrapbook Wizard; *Brads:* American Pin & Fastener; *Letters:* Hot Off The Press; *Computer fonts:* Texas Hero and Graverplate, downloaded from the Internet.

"Life"

SUPPLIES

Computer fonts: Papyrus, Texas Hero, John Hancock, Matisse, Batik, Carpenter ICG, Ordner, Antique Type, Graverplate, Boston, Cookie, Bambino, Arial and Arcana, downloaded from the Internet; *Bookplate:* Two Peas in a Bucket; *Rubber stamp and stamping ink:* Stampin' Up!; *Square punch:* Marvy Uchida; *Brads:* American Pin & Fastener.

"Delight"

SUPPLIES

Textured cardstock: Bazzill Basics; *Patterned paper:* 7 Gypsies; *Brads:* Doodlebug Design; *Postage stamps:* Limited Edition Rubber Stamps; *Definitions:* Making Memories and FoofaLa (black); *Computer font:* Texas Hero, downloaded from the Internet; *Other:* Ribbon and Chinese coins.

"Let's Play Pretend"

SUPPLIES
Textured cardstock: Bazzill Basics;
Rubber stamp: Stampin' Up!;
Stamping ink: VersaMark, Tsukineko;
Photo corners: Canson; *Tags:* Making
Memories; *Computer fonts:* Texas Hero
and Garamouche, downloaded from
the Internet; *Other:* Handmade paper,
jump rings, ribbon and screen wire.

Tyler has become such a "little girl". I've been surprised to learn how early pretend play begins. Yesterday afternoon, Tyler was having a great time playing with one of my purses and an old set of car keys that Grandma Morrow had given her. I was washing dishes when Tyler tapped me on the leg, held up one arm (she was using the other arm to keep her purse steady on her shoulder and to hold her car keys!) and said "Need hug?" After I gave her a big hug and kiss, she said "Bye-bye, Mommy" and headed to the garage door with her purse and keys! I almost always give Tyler and hug and kiss before I leave her...it's amazing the little things that children remember.

TIME booklet

When I turned 40, I realized I'd lived the equivalent of four decades. As I thought about my life, I discovered that each decade had its own unique and special moments. In my book, I chronicle the following moments from each 10-year span of my life:

1964–1974: Baby, Toddler, Playing, Growing, Learning

1974–1984: Teenager, Discovering, Young Adult

1984–1994: Young, Single, Working Hard, Playing Hard

1994–2004: Personal Growth, Introspection

I think it's important to take the time to reflect on who you are and where you've been. Consider creating a similar timeline of your life. Think about using this kind of booklet for other events in your life as well. How about a chronicle of your favorite vacations? Or a summary of your favorite things to do?

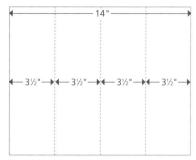

Step 1

Step 2

STEP-BY-STEP To make this booklet:

1. Start with a piece of 11" x 14" cardstock. (You'll have to piece together two pieces of cardstock.) Score the cardstock at 3½", 7" and 10½".

2. Fold at the score lines and burnish with a bone folder.

3. Decorate as desired.

Faye's Favorites

I like embellishments that are versatile enough to go with a variety of styles, photographs and themes. Here are a few of my favorite embellishments:

7 Gypsies (especially twill tape, photo turns and index plates) *www.7gypsies.com*

Li'l Davis Designs (especially round bookplates, keyholes, stencil alphabet and the bubble letters that fit the metal frames) *www.lildavisdesigns.com*

Making Memories (especially Simply Stated rub-ons and beaded chain) *www.makingmemories.com*

Watch Us (charms) *www.watchus.com*

Other
Chinese coins, watch faces, photo corners and compasses

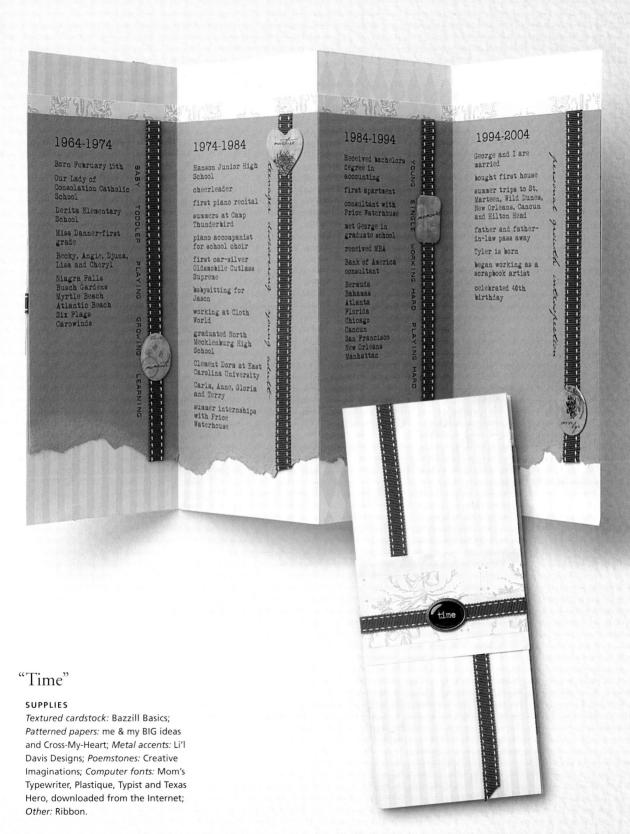

1964-1974

Born February 15th

Our Lady of
Consolation Catholic
School

Derita Elementary
School

Miss Danner-first
grade

Becky, Angie, Djuna,
Lisa and Cheryl

Niagra Falls
Busch Gardens
Myrtle Beach
Atlantic Beach
Six Flags
Carowinds

BABY TODDLER PLAYING GROWING LEARNING

1974-1984

Ranson Junior High
School

cheerleader

first piano recital

summers at Camp
Thunderbird

piano accoumpanist
for school choir

first car-silver
Oldsmobile Cutlass
Supreme

babysitting for
Jason

working at Cloth
World

graduated North
Mecklenburg High
School

Clement Dorm at East
Carolina University

Carla, Anne, Gloria
and Terry

summer internships
with Price
Waterhouse

nurture

teenager discovering young adult

1984-1994

Received bachelors
degree in
accounting

first apartment

consultant with
Price Waterhouse

met George in
graduate school

received MBA

Bank of America
consultant

Bermuda
Bahamas
Atlanta
Florida
Chicago
Cancun
San Francisco
New Orleans
Manhattan

YOUNG SINGLE WORKING HARD PLAYING HARD

memories

1994-2004

George and I are
married

bought first house

summer trips to St.
Marteen, Wild Dunes,
New Orleans, Cancun
and Hilton Head

father and father-
in-law pass away

Tyler is born

began working as a
scrapbook artist

celebrated 40th
birthday

mature family integration

time

"Time"

SUPPLIES
Textured cardstock: Bazzill Basics;
Patterned papers: me & my BIG ideas
and Cross-My-Heart; *Metal accents:* Li'l
Davis Designs; *Poemstones:* Creative
Imaginations; *Computer fonts:* Mom's
Typewriter, Plastique, Typist and Texas
Hero, downloaded from the Internet;
Other: Ribbon.

journaling INSPIRATION from magazines

I love *O, The Oprah Magazine.* My favorite column in her magazine is the last page—Oprah's "What I Know for Sure" article. When I receive my magazine each month, I always turn to the last page first. I generously "borrowed" the concept and format of her column as a tool to help me pause and give thought to what I know to be certain in our uncertain world.

What do you know for sure? What's on the final page of your favorite magazine? Does the final page inspire you to create a similar scrapbook layout?

F | what I know for sure

I love O, The Oprah Magazine. And my favorite column in her magazine is the last page - Oprah's "what I know for sure" article. When I receive my magazine each month, I always begin with the last page! I generously "borrowed" the concept and format of her column as a tool to help me pause and give thought to what I know to be certain in our uncertain world. Here's what I know for sure:

The mind is incredibly powerful. What you believe is what you will become.

Life is a journey, not a race.

Everything happens for a reason.

What you send into the world is what you'll receive back from the world. Sow kindness, you'll reap kindness. Sow negativity, you'll reap negativity.

Everyone has a calling and a purpose in life. We must make a job of figuring out what that calling is and then using it to improve our lives and the lives of others.

Life is a miracle.

God is in charge.

"You will receive from the world what you send into the world."

OCTOBER 6 2003

"What I Know for Sure"

SUPPLIES
Textured cardstock: Bazzill Basics; *Computer fonts:* Arial, Tahoma and Times New Roman, Microsoft Word; Book Antiqua, downloaded from the Internet.

JOURNALING the challenging times

"Delayed"

SUPPLIES

Textured cardstock: Bazzill Basics; *Metal frame, photo corners and letters:* Making Memories; *Concho:* Scrapworks; *Watch face:* 7 Gypsies; *Fern punch:* The Punch Bunch; *Computer fonts:* Mom's Typewriter, Ralph's Hand, Digiface and Trash, downloaded from the Internet; *Acrylic paint:* Plaid; *Other:* Ticket stubs and transparency. *Idea to note:* To create the border with the American Airlines logo, Faye copied the images from the web site and pasted them into a PowerPoint file.

Have you ever been in a situation that seemed like a comedy of errors? When I attended CKU-Utah in 2003, my flight was scheduled for an hour-and-15-minute layover in Dallas. Instead, I spent *five and a half* hours in Dallas enduring a comedy of airline errors, including mechanical problems, busy service teams, and flight attendants and pilots going "illegal" (which means they'd worked too many hours per FAA regulations).

The good news is that I finally made it safely to my destination. And, believe it or not, I used the time for sketching and journaling. In fact, I conceived this page sitting on a runway. The next time you're in a situation where you're delayed, take note of the various events going on around you. Who knows? You may find a slightly humorous twist to include in your scrapbook.

DESIGN TIP: See the airline logos printed on the left-hand side of my page? I found them on the American Airlines web site (*www.aa.com*), saved them to my computer and printed them onto my cardstock.

rag rug INSPIRATION

I find inspiration for my scrapbook pages everywhere! I love the look of this rag-tied rug in my laundry room. To create this look on my layout, I punched holes along the bottom and side of my cardstock. Then I cut and tied strips of pink-and-white gingham fabric through each hole.

"Play, Smile, Giggle"

SUPPLIES
Textured cardstock: Bazzill Basics; *Metal words:* Making Memories; *Computer fonts:* Texas Hero, downloaded from the Internet; Times New Roman, Microsoft Word; *Other:* Paint and fabric.

"Fashionista"

SUPPLIES

Textured cardstock: Bazzill Basics; *Patterned papers:* 7 Gypsies and Creative Imaginations; *Rickrack:* Wright's; *Label maker:* Dymo; *Brads:* American Pin & Fastener; *Computer font:* Ordner, downloaded from the Internet; *Other:* Fringe.

I left Tyler with her father for no more than an hour...and I returned to find a perfectly good pair of shoes ruined! George took Tyler to play with our 5-year old neighbor, Alex. This is the result of playing with sidewalk chalk on concrete in denim shoes!

"Tyler's Shoes"

SUPPLIES

Textured cardstock: Bazzill Basics; *Eyelets:* Doodlebug Design; *Rubber stamp:* Making Memories; *Stamping ink:* The Rubber Stamp Factory; *Computer font:* Ralph's Hand, downloaded from the Internet; *Other:* Safety pins, denim fabric, charms and beads.

PHOTOGRAPHY as inspiration

Photography is like a form of meditation to me. Without the viewfinder of my camera, I'm often guilty of just "looking." But there's nothing like framing a shot and really "seeing" your subject. Looking through the viewfinder causes me to slow down. I consider light, shadows and tones. I appreciate color, texture and angles.

I've discovered that when I stop and really see the world around me, I discover beauty in a variety of forms. I draw inspiration from my world, and I'm able to use that inspiration on my scrapbook pages. The next time you need a creative boost, consider picking up your camera and looking through the viewfinder. What do you "see" when you think about light, shadow, tones, color, texture and angles? How can you apply what you see to a scrapbook page?

To create this page, I simply folded a piece of black cardstock, cut out the "tab" on the top of the folder, decorated it with metal clips, and added the "Seeing 101" label on the tab. Think about creating your own interactive page folders for school pages (include artwork, a note from the teacher, an A+ test paper, school photographs), career pages (include your daily work schedule, positive comments from your boss, a business card), vacation pages (include postcards, brochures, a piece of hotel stationery, a restaurant napkin) and so on.

"Seeing 101"

SUPPLIES
Textured cardstock: Bazzill Basics; *Photo corners:* Canson; *Page pointers:* Antioch Publishing; *Brads:* American Pin & Fastener and Making Memories; *Mesh:* The Robin's Nest Press; *Eyelets:* Doodlebug Design; *Label maker:* Dymo; *Computer fonts:* Texas Hero, Graverplate and Mom's Typewriter, downloaded from the Internet; *Other:* Staples, bulldog clip, jewelry tag and torn film cartons.

"Photography 101"

SUPPLIES
Textured paper: Bazzill Basics; *Patterned papers:* Frances Meyer and Paper Pizazz; *Buttons:* Dress It Up; *Computer fonts:* Scriptina and Arcana, downloaded from the Internet; Tahoma, Microsoft Word.

favorite COLORS

Green has been my favorite color for more years than I can remember. It's cool, it's calming, and it's serene. I love the deep forest greens of the holidays as much as I enjoy the pale mossy green color of my family room. Because green is so dominant in nature, it also reminds me of life and growth and good health.

On this scrapbook page, I celebrate my favorite color using a variety of techniques. To build this "green" page, I used five different shades of green cardstock, two green ribbons, two green stamps and two green labels. A fun design note? I used foam dots to pop different elements off my page.

What's your favorite color? Why does it appeal to you? How can you use your favorite color as inspiration for a scrapbook page?

"Green"

SUPPLIES

Textured cardstock: Bazzill Basics; *Rubber stamps:* Rubber Stampede and All Night Media, *Stamping ink:* Brilliance, Tsukineko; *Postage stamps:* Limited Edition Rubber Stamps and me & my BIG ideas; *Ephemera:* Design Originals and Collage Joy; *Pen:* Zig Writer, EK Success; *Computer fonts:* Mom's Typewriter, Top Secret, Rubber Stamp, Arcana Manuscript, Ordner, Antique Type, MA Sexy, Graverplate, Texas Hero and Papyrus, downloaded from the Internet; Tahoma, Microsoft Word; CK Inky and CK Chemistry, "Fresh Fonts" CD, *Creating Keepsakes; Other:* Ribbon.

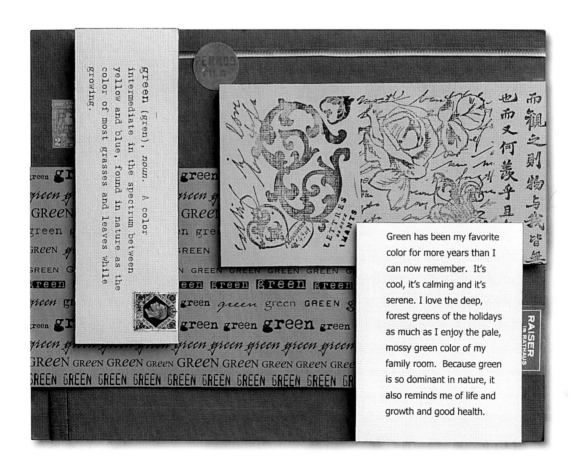

"Flower Garden"

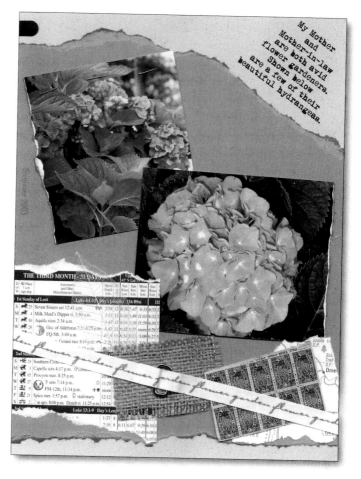

SUPPLIES

Textured cardstock: Bazzill Basics; *Patterned paper:* Paper Pizazz; *Trading stamps:* Collage Joy; *Skeletonized leaf:* The Lacey Paper Company; *Book dart:* Antioch Publishing; *Date stamp:* Making Memories; *Stamping ink:* Susan Branch, Colorbök; *Twill tape:* Wright's; *Rectangle nickel slide:* 7 Gypsies; *Computer fonts:* Mom's Typewriter and Carpenter, downloaded from the Internet; *Other:* Burlap, staples and page from an almanac.

Faye's Favorites

COLORS	PATTERNED PAPERS	COMPUTER FONTS
Black	**7 Gypsies**	**Garamouche**
Gray	*www.7gypsies.com*	*www.fonts.com*
Green	**Design Originals**	**Graverplate**
Red	*www.d-originals.com*	Microsoft Word

BAZZILL BASICS CARDSTOCK COLORS

Avocado	**K & Company**	**Texas Hero**
Celadon	*www.kandcompany.com*	*www.scrapvillage.com*
Driftwood	**Li'l Davis Designs**	**Top Secret**
Fog	*www.lildavisdesigns.com*	Available on the Internet
Paper Bag		

MIXED MEDIA ARTISTS

Nina Bagley
www.itsmysite.com/ninabagleydesign

Beth Cote
www.alteredbook.com

Claudine Hellmuth
www.collageartist.com

EPHEMERA SOURCES

Collage Joy
www.collagejoy.com

Limited Edition Rubber Stamps
www.limitededitionrs.com

Manto Fev
www.mantofev.com

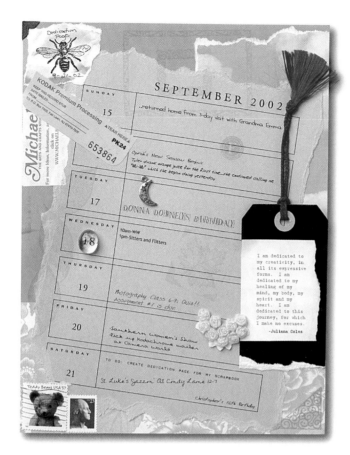

"September 2002"

SUPPLIES

Textured cardstock: Bazzill Basics; *Patterned papers:* Anna Griffin and Paper Pizazz; *Rubber stamps:* Anita's; *Stamping ink:* Anita's; VersaMark, Tsukineko; *Tag:* DMD, Inc.; *Flower embellishment:* Jolee's by You, EK Success; *Charm:* Watch Us; *Pen:* Zig Writer, EK Success; *Computer fonts:* Garamouche, Graverplate, Wayne's Hand, Hanford's Hand, Trasks Hand, Ticket Capitals, Trebuchet, Patricia's Hand, Gail's Hand, Ordner, Wendy's Hand and Batik, downloaded from the Internet; *Other:* Tassel, postage stamp, foam stamp, page pebble and ephemera.

"100 Things I Love"

SUPPLIES

Patterned paper: me & my BIG ideas; *Vellum:* The Write Stock; *Computer fonts:* CK Cursive, "The Best of Creative Lettering" CD Vol. 2, *Creating Keepsakes;* 2Peas Unforgettable, downloaded from *www.twopeasinabucket.com;* Yippy Skippy, Zonker's Hand, Maraca and Matisse, downloaded from the Internet; PK Ralph's Hand, package unknown; *Die cut:* Cross-My-Heart; "T" and "I" *letter stickers:* Source unknown.

"Memo"

SUPPLIES

Vellum envelopes: The Write Stock; *Charms:* Watch Us; *Beaded chain:* Making Memories; *Computer font:* Times New Roman, Microsoft Word; *Other:* Green ledger paper.

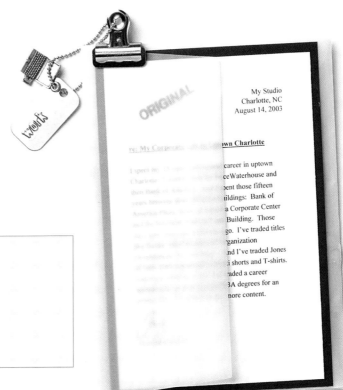

The open flap of one envelope is glued to the front of the adjacent envelope.

Photography

Adopt the pace of nature.
Her secret is patience.
-Emerson

I HAVE HAD A WONDERFUL TIME TAKING PHOTOGRAPHY 260 AT CPCC THIS FALL! Photography 260 is the introductory photography course that teaches theory as well as basic photographic techniques. My instructor, John Hilarides, is a professional photographer with an emphasis on architectural photography. He is also a visual arts director at The Levine Museum of The New South in uptown Charlotte.

I love black and white photography, but I've never been pleased with the prints that I shoot. Although this class does not focus on black and white photography, I knew that the principles would help improve the quality of my black and white prints as well.

My most important "learnings"? Understanding the principles of light and its impact on photos; how shutter speed and aperture interact and how to shoot high contrast photos. Little did I know that I'm often shooting high contrast scenes when metering African Americans against light backgrounds! And I am very comfortable with all of the features of my camera...a Canon Rebel EOS which I bought for the class. Learning and using all of the features was a key objective for this class.

My biggest surprise? How much I've invested in the class monetarily as well as in time! We shot and processed at least one roll of chrome (slide) film each week which is more expensive than print film. Additionally we needed a telephoto lens and we had assignments which required get a digital scan from a slide and cutting mat board!

I love the black and white pictures shown here...I really think my *eye* is beginning to develop!

Faye

FAYE MORROW BELL

These pictures were taken in the Derita Community where I grew up. The leaves were taken in my mother's backyard. The ducks and the pond are common "Morrow" property across the street from my childhood home.

"Photography"

SUPPLIES

Textured cardstock: Bazzill Basics; *Computer fonts:* Texas Hero, downloaded from the Internet; Arial and Times New Roman, Microsoft Word.

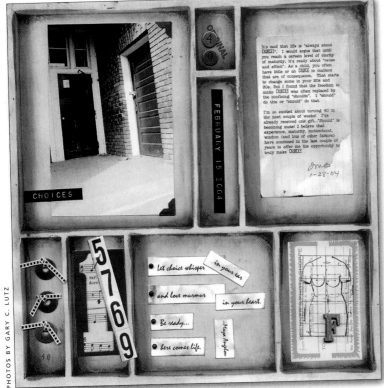

"Choices"

SUPPLIES

Patterned papers: Karen Foster Design and Li'l Davis Designs; *Ribbon, washers, staple and "40" stamp:* Making Memories; *Computer fonts:* Mistral, Typist and Top Secret, downloaded from the Internet; *Ephemera:* Design Originals; *Stamping ink:* StazOn, Tsukineko; Stampin' Up!; *Female torso rubber stamp:* A Stamp in the Hand; *"Original" rubber stamp:* Office Depot; *Brads:* Doodlebug Design; *"F" letter:* Li'l Davis Designs; *Photo corners:* Canson; *Chalk:* EK Success; *Pen:* Zig Writer, EK Success; *Other:* Label maker, index cards and walnut ink.

notes

I always tab pages of
interest in my idea books.
Use this space to make notes
and references to the ideas
that you'll incorporate into
your scrapbook.

notes